The Works Of Daniel Defoe...: Due Preparation For The Plague, As Well For Soul As Body

being some seasonable Thoughts upon the visible approach

Daniel Defoe

of the present dreadful contagion in France, the properest measures to prevent it, and the great work of submitting to it. Psal. xci. 10. "There shall no evil befal thee, neither shall no Plague come nigh thy dwelling." London: printed for E. Matthews at the Bible, and J. Batley at the Dove, in Paternoster Row, 1722, 12mo."

Intro - 10 pages
Work - 272 pages

Nabu Public Domain Reprints:

You are holding a reproduction of an original work published before 1923 that is in the public domain in the United States of America, and possibly other countries. You may freely copy and distribute this work as no entity (individual or corporate) has a copyright on the body of the work. This book may contain prior copyright references, and library stamps (as most of these works were scanned from library copies). These have been scanned and retained as part of the historical artifact.

This book may have occasional imperfections such as missing or blurred pages, poor pictures, errant marks, etc. that were either part of the original artifact, or were introduced by the scanning process. We believe this work is culturally important, and despite the imperfections, have elected to bring it back into print as part of our continuing commitment to the preservation of printed works worldwide. We appreciate your understanding of the imperfections in the preservation process, and hope you enjoy this valuable book.

THE WORKS OF
DANIEL DEFOE

IN SIXTEEN VOLUMES

LIMITED TO ONE THOUSAND
REGISTERED SETS, OF WHICH
THIS IS NUMBER 681

THE SISTER COMFORTS HER BROTHER

Dear brother, I am very sorry to see you in this melancholy, discouraged condition

THE WORKS OF DANIEL DEFOE
VOLUME FIFTEEN

DUE PREPARATIONS
FOR
THE PLAGUE
AS WELL FOR SOUL AS BODY

WITH THE AUTHOR'S PREFACE, AND AN INTRODUCTION BY
G. H. MAYNADIER, Ph.D.
DEPARTMENT OF ENGLISH, HARVARD UNIVERSITY

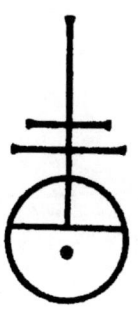

NEW YORK
THE JENSON SOCIETY
MCMV

Copyright, 1904, by
THE UNIVERSITY PRESS

UNIVERSITY PRESS · JOHN WILSON
AND SON, CAMBRIDGE, U.S.A.

CONTENTS

	PAGE
INTRODUCTION	ix
AUTHOR'S INTRODUCTION	xvii
DUE PREPARATIONS FOR THE PLAGUE	1
THE DUMB PHILOSOPHER; GREAT BRITAIN'S WONDER	207
The Preface	209
The Dumb Philosopher	211
A TRUE RELATION OF THE APPARITION OF ONE MRS. VEAL	249
The Preface	251
A Relation of the Apparition of Mrs. Veal	253
THE DESTRUCTION OF THE ISLE OF ST. VINCENT	267

LIST OF ILLUSTRATIONS

THE SISTER COMFORTS HER BROTHER . . . *Frontispiece*

WHEN THE PLAGUE BEGAN TO ABATE . . . ,, 80

INTRODUCTION

*D*UE *Preparations for the Plague, as well for Soul as Body*, was published in 1722. Whether it came out before or after the *Journal of the Plague Year*, which appeared in March of the same year, cannot be definitely said. Though Mr. Lee accidentally omitted the *Due Preparations* from the catalogue of Defoe's works prefixed to the first volume of his *Daniel Defoe*, there can be little doubt that the book was from Defoe's pen. It was on a subject which we know, from *A Journal of the Plague Year*, greatly interested him; and portions of the book deal with incidents mentioned in the better known *Journal*. Besides, as Mr. Aitken has shown,[1] *Due Preparations for the Plague* is full of Defoe's mannerisms, both in vocabulary and in narrative method. "Neither — or" is an instance of the former; the use of dialogue in the second part, of the latter. There seems to be no good reason for doubting Defoe's authorship.

It is commonly said that Defoe wrote *Due Preparations for the Plague* for the same purpose as *A Journal of the Plague Year*, namely to rouse people to take precautions against the plague which had

---

[1] Introduction to Vol. XV., *Romances and Narratives by Daniel Defoe*, — London, 1901.

INTRODUCTION

been raging in Marseilles in 1720 and 1721. That Defoe was actuated somewhat by public-spirited motives in writing his two works on the plague is likely, but it is even likelier that he was led to compose them by his shrewd commercial sense. He was aware that the interest in the Marseilles plague would give them a good sale.

Due Preparations for the Plague reads for the most part like a continuation of the more famous *Journal of the Plague Year*. Showing what preparations, both spiritual and material, should be made for the disease, by instances cited from the Great Plague, it becomes very much like the *Journal* in tone, though it is not so evenly interesting. A reader's interest cannot but flag in the second part, when he struggles with the tedious religious cant of the sister who warns her brother to be spiritually ready for the pestilence. In some of the verbose, unnatural conversation here, Defoe appears at his worst. When a reader, however, comes to the story of the sister's taking refuge from the pestilence with her two brothers on a ship which drops down the Thames, his interest revives. And nothing in the *Journal* itself is better narrative than the story, in the first part of *Due Preparations*, of the family "in the parish of St. Alban's, Wood Street," who, in order to escape the sickness, lived shut up in their house, without once going out, from the fourteenth of July to the first of December.

Immediately following *Due Preparations for the Plague* will be found a short history with a very long title, namely:— *The Dumb Philosopher: or, Great*

INTRODUCTION

Britain's Wonder, containing I. A Faithful and very Surprising Account, how Dickory Cronke, a Tinner's Son, in the County of Cornwall, was born Dumb, and continued so for 58 years; and how, some Days before he Died, he came to his Speech. With Memoirs of his Life, and the manner of his Death. II. A Declaration of his Faith and Principles in Religion: With a Collection of Select Meditations composed in his Retirement. III. His Prophetical Observations upon the Affairs of Europe, more particularly of Great Britain, from 1720 to 1729. The whole extracted from his original Papers, and confirmed by unquestionable authority. To which is annexed, His Elegy, written by a young Cornish Gentleman, of Exeter Coll. in Oxford. With an Epitaph by another Hand.

This curious pamphlet was published in October, 1719, nearly a year and a half after the subject of it, according to Defoe's statement, had died. It is probable that the history was founded on fact. Dickory Cronke was very likely a real man like Duncan Campbell and the criminals whose lives are sketched in the volume which is to follow this. He did not achieve the notoriety of any of these, however. On the contrary, he lived obscurely in Wales or the southwest of England, and his reputation may be supposed to have been purely local. For this reason, unlike his contemporary dumb man, Campbell, who for years was a much visited fortune-teller of the metropolis, Dickory Cronke died unknown to fame. There is no mention of him in either contemporary periodicals or the *Dictionary of National Biography*; and

INTRODUCTION

in 1901, such a careful student of Defoe as Mr. G. A. Aitken had been unable to get any information about him.

The Elegy and the Epitaph at the end of the history are as likely to have been Defoe's as the work of " a young Cornish Gentleman " of Exeter College, or of the gentleman, who, having " heard much in commendation " of the dumb man, was said to have written his epitaph. At all events, the verses which Defoe wrote on *The Character of the late Dr. Samuel Annesley, by Way of Elegy* in 1697 are much like those on Cronke, as a few lines will show: —

> " A Heavenly Patience did his Mind possess,
>   Cheerful in Pain and thoughtful in Distress;
> Mighty in Works of Sacred Charity,
>   Which none knew better how to guide than he;
> Bounty and generous thoughts took up his Mind,
> Extensive, like his Maker's, to Mankind."

The old graveyards of New England can show many epitaphs neither better nor worse than this.

Following *The Dumb Philosopher*, will be found two interesting bits of narrative by Defoe: — *A True Relation of the Apparition of one Mrs. Veal, the next Day after her Death, to one Mrs. Bargrave at Canterbury, the 8th of September, 1705. Which Apparition recommends the Perusal of Drelincourt's Book of Consolations against the Fears of Death*, and *The Destruction of the Isle of St. Vincent*. The former of these is one of the best known compositions of Defoe. From the time that Scott[1] selected it as a

---
[1] *Biographical Memoirs: Daniel DeFoe.*

INTRODUCTION

good example of Defoe's power of imparting reality to his narratives, it has been especially famous, and deservedly so; though apparently it does not show Defoe's inventive powers so much as Scott thought.

Scott mentions an old tradition to the effect that Defoe wrote the *Apparition* as a puff for Drelincourt's book of *Consolations against the Fears of Death*, and he calls it an instance of Defoe's bold invention that he " summoned up a ghost from the grave to bear witness in favour of a halting body of divinity." It is a pity that nowadays doubt attaches to this story of Defoe's writing a puff for Drelincourt's book, for it is exactly what he would have been likely to do. Mr. Lee, however, in his *Daniel Defoe*,[1] argues that *Mrs. Veal* was written for no such purpose. Drelincourt's book, he states, was in no need of such a puff. The third edition sold very well, but the fourth, which contained a reprint of Defoe's *Apparition*, was slow in selling. After this the *Apparition of Mrs. Veal* was sometimes printed with Drelincourt's book and sometimes not, till the eleventh edition, from which, to the present time, according to Lee, " Drelincourt has never been published without it." For my part, I do not feel that this testimony entirely disproves the old story. On the other hand, it proves that from the first, there was some connection between Defoe's pamphlet and Drelincourt. The fact that the first edition of Drelincourt which included the *Apparition* did not sell so well as a previous edition without the *Apparition*, proves not that Defoe did not write his pamphlet partly for a

[1] London, 1869, Vol. I., page 127.

INTRODUCTION

puff, but rather that the puff was not successful. And though Drelincourt's book is not the only one which the ghost of Mrs. Veal recommends to Mrs. Bargrave, fully twice as much space is given to this as to the book next most commended, Norris's *Friendship in Perfection*, and much more praise. After all, may it not have occurred to Defoe, as he wrote *The Apparition of Mrs. Veal*, that in telling a remarkable contemporary story, he might incidentally do Drelincourt some service?

That *Mrs. Veal* was a contemporary story now seems clear; we are no longer to accept it as a marvellous instance of Defoe's power of invention. A few readers to-day will believe that Mrs. Bargrave actually saw the apparition which Defoe described; a great many more will believe the whole thing to have been an hallucination. However that may be, Mr. Aitken[1] has proved that the remarkable story was current when Defoe's *Apparition* was published, and that it was told of real people. There were two families of Bargraves in Canterbury at the time, to either of which Mrs. Veal's friend might have belonged. There were also Watsons in Canterbury. At Dover, there was a William Veal who was Comptroller of the Customs in 1719, and therefore, as Defoe said, may well have had a place in the Custom House in 1705. What is more, according to the Parish register of St. Mary's, Dover, a Mrs. Veal was buried on the tenth of September, 1705; that is,

[1] *Defoe's Apparition of Mrs. Veal, Nineteenth Century*, January, 1895; and introduction to the 15th vol. of *Romances and Narratives by Daniel Defoe*. J. M. Dent, London, 1901.

INTRODUCTION

three days after her death as stated by Defoe. And finally Mr. Aitken has found evidence of an interview with Mrs. Bargrave in a note at the beginning of a copy of the *Apparition* published with an edition of Drelincourt about 1710, — a note which states that the writer talked with Mrs. Bargrave "on May 21, 1714," and learned from her that everything in Defoe's account of the *Apparition* was substantially true.

Though all this proves Defoe to have made use of little invention in *Mrs. Veal*, it does not prove that the persuasive reality of the story is not due to his way of telling it. Any one who attempts to write out a prosy conversation like that between Mrs. Veal's supposed ghost and Mrs. Bargrave will soon discover the difficulty in making it seem real.

It has commonly been supposed of Defoe, as of all great writers, that he took most of the situations of his stories ready-made, spending his inventive force chiefly on the detail. This late discovery about the source of *Mrs. Veal* shows that even detail he would take ready-made, when he could find it. Possibly he did so more than we have hitherto believed. If so, his rapid productiveness, though still astonishing, would not be quite so marvellous as it has seemed.

If *Mrs. Veal*, on the whole, is a story which shows little of Defoe's invention, *The Destruction of the Isle of St. Vincent*, which concludes this volume, seems to show a great deal. It is possible that Defoe made this up out of whole cloth. On the other hand, some rumour of the destruction of the island may

INTRODUCTION

have reached him, which he would not scruple to elaborate into a sensational newspaper article. Accordingly, on July 5th, 1718, there appeared in *Mist's Journal*, the Jacobite periodical with which Defoe connected himself in 1717, the amazing story of the destruction of the island. It is interesting to-day for two reasons. It shows what Defoe's imagination could do, when he gave it full swing; and it is remarkable for its many resemblances to the authentic stories of the frightful disaster at St. Pierre, Martinique, in May, 1902. The volcano of Mount Pelée then actually did what Defoe imagined the island of St. Vincent to do on the twenty-sixth of March, 1718.

The only retraction of Defoe's circumstantial fabrication about the destruction of St. Vincent was the following notice in *Mist's Journal* for August 2, 1718.

"*The Island of St. Vincent Not Destroyed.*

They pretend to tell us a strange Story, viz., that the Island of St. Vincent is found again, and is turn'd into a Volcano, or burning Mountain; but we must acknowledge we do not believe one word of it."

G. H. MAYNADIER

AUTHOR'S INTRODUCTION

BEFORE I enter upon the subject of preparation for so terrible a visitation as this of the plague, it is meet I should say something of the reasons we have to be apprehensive of it in this nation. If the reasons of our fears are not good, the seasonableness of the whole work will be called in question, and it may be looked on as an officious prophesying of evil tidings. To talk of preparation for a danger which we are not in danger of would be a needless alarming the people, and is a thing oftentimes attended with ill consequences to the public, being injurious to commerce, to credit, and to the civil peace.

Blessed be God, the evil is yet at a distance, and the danger may be said to be remote; but as we (1) find it to be a terrible spreading distemper, furious and raging beyond what was ever known in this country, sweeping away old and young till it has desolated whole towns and even some populous cities; (2) that it spreads apace this way, having already advanced itself above 100 miles in these eight months past, and that we have some reason to believe that it was come much nearer than they allowed us to know of; on these accounts, I think, it is reasonable at least to put ourselves in a posture not to be surprised if we should meet with the same here.

AUTHOR'S INTRODUCTION

Besides, I am far from being singular in my apprehensions; the Government are evidently in the same concern; and therefore we have had several Proclamations, Orders of Council, and other directions for ships performing quarantine, and for goods to be opened and aired which come from suspected places; and one Act of Parliament has been passed to enforce those orders upon the highest penalties, nay, even upon pain of death. And so cautious was the Parliament in this point that they put the nation to the expense of £25,000 sterling to burn two Turkish ships which were but suspected to have goods on board which might contain an infection, and which might bring the plague among us, which £25,000 has been paid to the merchants and owners of the ships and cargo in satisfaction of the damages done them.

Can any man say that the Government have not had occasion for these measures? Let such look to what has been done in Holland, where they not only burned two ships, but hanged a man for attempting to save some goods out of the wreck of one ship that was cast away, and which should otherwise have been burnt as coming from places infected or supposed to be infected with the plague.

Now, while we receive daily such afflicting and melancholy accounts from abroad of the spreading of the plague and of its approaches this way, and find not only private persons but even the Government itself, and neighbouring Governments also, justly alarmed, who can be wholly unconcerned about it? Certain it is, that if it proceeds much farther, noth-

AUTHOR'S INTRODUCTION

ing but the distinguishing goodness of God can be said to keep it from reaching hither, the intercourse of commerce and the many necessary occasions of passing and repassing between the two kingdoms being so great, and a full stop of that intercourse being so many ways impracticable, as we see it is.

If, then, we are in expectation and under just apprehension of it, what appearance is there of our preparations for it? Never less, I think, was to be seen in any nation under heaven, whether we speak of preparations to avoid and escape it, or of preparations to wait and expect it; whether we speak of preparations for the soul or for the body. And this alone has been the occasion of writing this book.

We have, indeed, some physicians who have given their opinions in the matter of our managing ourselves with respect to medicine, in case of the plague breaking out among us, and unto this purpose they treat a little (though very superficially) of the nature of the disease, the best preventive remedies, &c. But even in this part, however (as I said, superficial at best), yet they differ with, contradict, and oppose one another, and leave their readers as uncertain and dissatisfied, as far to seek, and at a loss for their conduct, as they were before.

As to the other part, and what we should think of doing when we set such an awful providence in a clear light before us, with respect to our religious preparations, and for our meeting and submitting ourselves to all the dispensations of Providence of what kind soever, which, doubtless, is the duty of every

AUTHOR'S INTRODUCTION

Christian — of this, indeed, I have seen, I may say, nothing at all offered in public; on the contrary, the whole world is intent and busy on their ordinary occasions. Men pursue the usual course of the world; they push their interest, their gain, or their pleasures and gaiety with the same gust, or rather more than ever. Nay, the cry of the nation's follies grows louder and louder every day, and so far we are from considering that, when God's judgments are abroad in the earth, the inhabitants should learn righteousness, that we are rather learning to be more superficially wicked than ever; witness the increase of plays and playhouses, one being now building, though so many already in use; witness the public trading and stock-jobbing on the Sabbath day; witness the raging avarice of the times, by which the civil interest of the nation is ruined and destroyed; witness also our feuds, divisions, and heats, as well in religious differences as those that are political, which are all carried up to dreadful extremes.

Upon these many accounts this work has been set on foot, which, though in the design of it 't is calculated for the present particular occasion of the terrors we are under about the plague, which I may very well call impending, yet may be useful many ways, both to us and to posterity, though we should be spared from that portion of this bitter cup which I verily believe is reserved for us.

To make this discourse familiar and agreeable to every reader, I have endeavoured to make it as historical as I could, and have therefore intermingled it with some accounts of fact, where I could come at

AUTHOR'S INTRODUCTION

them, and some by report, suited to and calculated for the moral, endeavouring by all possible and just methods to encourage the great work of preparation, which is the main end of this undertaking.

The cases I have stated here are suited with the utmost care to the circumstances past, and more especially as they are reasonably supposed to suit those to come; and as I very particularly remember the last visitation of this kind which afflicted this nation in 1665, and have had occasion to converse with many other persons who lived in this city all the while, I have chosen some of their cases as precedents for our present instructions. I take leave so far to personate the particular people in their histories as is needful to the case in hand without making use of their names, though in many cases I could have descended to the very names and particulars of the persons themselves.

But 't is the example that is the thing aimed at. The application to the same measures is argued from the reason and nature of the thing as well as from the success, and I recommend the experiments said here to be made no farther than they appear rational and just, with whatever success they have been practised. As to the religious history here mentioned, till I see some just exception raised against the pattern laid before us in every part of it, I cannot suggest there will lie any against the manner of relating it, and for that reason I make no apology for that part, but proceed direct to the work itself.

DUE PREPARATIONS FOR THE PLAGUE,

AS WELL FOR SOUL AS BODY

DUE PREPARATIONS FOR THE PLAGUE

PERHAPS my method in the preparations I am now to speak of may be something singular; but I hope they shall not be the less profitable. I shall make no more introductions. I divide my subject into two generals:—

1. Preparations against the Plague.
2. Preparations for the Plague.

The first of these I call preparations for the body. The second I call preparations for the soul.

Both, I hope, may be useful for both, and especially the first shall be subservient to the last.

1. Preparations against the Plague; and these I divide into (1) General, Public, and National Preparations, namely, for keeping it out of the country or city or town we live in, and preventing its spreading and penetrating from one place to another; the measures which are now taking, being, I must needs say, very deficient; and (2) Particular Preparations, such as relate to persons and families for preserving us from infection in our houses, when it pleases God that it shall come into the city, or place wherein we live.

General preparations seem to be confined to the measures which the Government or magistrates may take to preserve the people from infection. The main thing the Government seem to have their eyes upon in this nation is to limit and prohibit commerce with places infected, and restrain the importation of such goods as are subject to be infected; here it is granted that some goods are apt more than others to retain the poisonous effluvia which they may have received in foreign parts, and, by consequence, are apt to emit those effluvias again when they arrive here and come to be spread. These poisonous or infectious effluvia, or particles, as some call them, take hold or seize upon the people who are handling them. I need not enumerate the particular sorts of goods which are thus esteemed susceptible of infection. Abundance has been said on that subject by other authors, and all our proclamations, Acts of Parliament, &c., which have been passed on this subject, have taken notice of them.

It is true that, as I have hinted before, our Government have seemed sufficiently careful to settle such limitations of commerce, prohibitions, and quarantines as have been necessary to be observed by ships and passengers coming into his Majesty's dominions, with respect to the places suspected as well as to such as are known to be now visited, and also to extend those limitations and restrictions to more places and ports as they have thought fit, and as the infection has been found to advance nearer and nearer; and had the injunctions thus laid on our people been punctually and duly observed, possibly we might with some ground have been encouraged to hope for deliverance, or at least to have flattered our-

[margin note: Belief the plague was in the air]

selves with a possibility of guarding our principal places against it.

But I must not omit that we are not a nation qualified so well to resist the progress of such a distemper, or the entrance of it into our country, as others are. We have a set of men among us so bent upon their gain, by that we call clandestine trade, that they would even venture to import the plague itself if they were to get by it, and so give it to all that lived near them, not valuing the gross and horrid injustice that they do to other people. What a man ventures for himself is nothing, because it is his own act and deed; but what he ventures for others is the worst of violence upon them, and perhaps, in such a case as this, is the worst sort of murder.

This vice in our commerce is introduced by the necessity this nation has been in of clogging foreign trade with heavy duties and imports, which gives encouragement to smugglers and runners of goods to venture at all hazards to bring such goods in upon us privately, and these men, I doubt I may say without injuring them, value not what the goods are or whence they come, so they can but bring them on shore free of the duties and imports I speak of. We have examples of this before us, which justifies the charge, and I need say no more to prove it.

The preparations against the plague in this case must be the work of the Government. It is confessed that this is a difficulty even to the Government itself, and it will be hard to say what they can do more than is done effectually to prevent this dreadful trade; and without some very great severity, I believe it will never be done; and yet till it is done we cannot pretend to take effectual measures in this nation for preventing the plague coming among us.

The physicians seem at present to fall in with the French methods, viz., of preventing the spreading of infection by surrounding the towns where it shall happen to be with troops of soldiers, cutting off all communication with the countries or parts of the country where such towns are that shall be infected. This Dr. Mead has been pleased to propose also in his treatise called " A Short Discourse."

I must confess I do not see that this can be made practicable in England, and we see already it has not been effectual in France, notwithstanding greater severities have been used there than I presume will ever be allowed to be used here. For example, the plague began in Provence, in a part of the country the most easily separated from the rest of the world of any that can be singled out on their side, as will appear by the situation of the country. The south part of Provence, or, as some call it, the Lower Provence, is surrounded by water on three sides, and by the unpassable mountains of Piedmont and Nice on the fourth side; that is to say, it is bounded by the sea from the said mountains to the mouth of the great river Rhone, on the south; on the west it is bounded by the said river Rhone to the mouth of the Durance, on the south side of the district of Avignon; and on the north it is bounded by the said river Durance, to the mouth of the river

PREPARATIONS FOR THE PLAGUE

Verdon, and thence by the river Verdon to the foot of the said mountains of Piedmont.

On the south side, 't is allowed, there needed no guard, and the nature of the thing armed all the world from receiving any vessel coming from Provence, or suffering the people out of them to land; and if I am not misinformed, several people that did put to sea (as it were desperate from thence) are still missing, and it is believed have perished at sea, having not been allowed to set their feet on shore in any part of the world.

On the side of the river Rhone the west banks of the river have been so well guarded that nothing has been able to pass; and though the islands in the mouth of the Rhone have been infected, the distressed people of Arles, having almost by force gotten out among them at La Canourgue, Salon, and other places, yet the river being great and the navigation of it wholly stopped, the distemper has been kept off on that side.

On the east side also the mountains and the frontiers of Nice have been so well guarded by the troops of Piedmont, and the passes of those mountains are so few, so difficult, and so easy to be closed up, that very few of the people have attempted to escape that way, and those that have attempted it have been fired at and driven back, or if pressing forward have been killed.

But on the north side the case has been quite different, for the Durance and the Verdon are smaller rivers, and in many places fordable; so that in spite of all the guards placed in their lines, and the vigilance of the patrols on the bank of the river, men have made their escape in the dark, and by private ways have gotten into the mountains, and from thence, being acquainted with the country, have passed on from place to place till they have found retreats, and have been received by their friends, and concealed as they desired. Some indeed have been discovered and have been driven back, and others have been killed; but certain it is, that among the many of these desperate people which have thus got away, some have been touched with the contagion — nay, some that perhaps have thought themselves sound and in health, and these have carried it with them to the places where they have made their retreat.

Thus a galley slave who made his escape from Marseilles, and, as it is said, reached to his brother's house at La Canourgue in the Gavandan, carried the plague with him; and thus it broke out at once one hundred and forty miles off Marseilles, and all the precautions, guards, lines, patrols, &c., used to prevent its coming out of the Nether Provinces, were at once defeated.

By the same accident it has spread itself in the Gavandan from one village to another, and from one town to another, till, as by the last account we are told, above an hundred villages and towns are visited in that part of the country, and the infection is spread into the Vivarais on one side, the diocese of Uzes on another, the province of Auvergne on a third, and into Rouergue on a fourth side, and yet at all these places the towns infected are immediately invested, and all communication with them cut off as soon

PREPARATIONS FOR THE PLAGUE

as it is known they are infected, and all the other regulations observed which are directed by the Government there.

This now is the effect of surrounding of towns with lines and with soldiers, and imprisoning the people against their will, forbidding the sound separating themselves from the sick, which they must needs take for an insufferable cruelty, and by which means they make the people desperate and mad. So that rather than stay in the place to be poisoned with the breath of dying people, and be certainly infected with the stench of bodies dead or sick of the plague, they venture at all hazards to make their escape, and, in effecting this, infect their friends; and thus it will be among us, I doubt not, if ever such methods are put in practice here.

Besides, as they can have no pretence to invest a town, or prohibit the inhabitants from quitting it, till it is infected, they put those inhabitants upon all possible means of concealing the infection when it is begun, till those who are in the secret of it can make their escape; and thus they travel securely with the distemper upon them, and emit the effluvia of infection wherever they come. Thus the city of Avignon was infected a month and seven days, viz., from the 17th of August to the 23rd of September, before it was publicly known in the country round; so that people went freely into the city from all the villages about Avignon, and the citizens went freely out into the country, and the distemper was fetched by one and carried by the other, without any precaution to all the neighbouring towns for several leagues round the place, several of which towns are more fatally touched with the contagion than the city itself, as Bedarrides and Sorgues on the north, Barbantine on the south, and even at length the city of Orange itself; and now they are obliged to quit the old lines and post on the bank of the river Durance, and to draw a new line near a hundred miles in length, to wit, from St. Paul Trois Châteaux on the Rhone to Montbron east, and from thence down to Lauris on the Durance on the south, and so on the bank of that river to its fall into the Rhone west; and yet all these lines seem not to be capable to effect the thing proposed by them, for when the inhabitants are thus made desperate by locking up the sound with the sick, they do and will find ways to escape, whatever hazards it may be to themselves or others.

Whereas, if the people were left at their liberty, except as was practised here in the time of the last visitation, viz., by shutting up houses known to be infected, — I say, if the people were left at liberty, those that did flee at all, would flee because they were infected, and thereby save their lives, and likewise not carry the distemper with them when they went.

In the next place, the cutting off of the communication of one part of the country with another in England would be such a general interruption of trade, that it would entirely ruin the countries and towns so cut off, and the people would be very tumultuous and uneasy upon that head.

It seems to me a much more rational method, that as soon as any town or village appears to be

PREPARATIONS FOR THE PLAGUE

visited, all the sound people of the town be immediately removed and obliged to go to some certain particular place, where barracks should be built for them, or tents pitched for them, and where they should be obliged to perform a quarantine of days, and after that to be admitted to go whither they pleased, except back to the town from whence they came; if they thought fit to remain where they were till the town or village infected was entirely restored, and had been so for a full quarantine, then they might be admitted again; and if any families proved to have the distemper in their encampment, they should remove again, leaving the sick families behind. And thus continually moving the sound from the sick, the distemper would abate, of course, and the contagion be less strong by how much fewer persons were affected with it.

Nothing is more certain than that the contagion strengthens, and the infectious particles in the air, if any such there are, increase in quantity, as the greater number of sick bodies are kept together. The effluvia emitted from the bodies infected are more rank and more contagious, and are carried farther in the air the more bodies are infected, and are therefore more apt to be received from house to house; and were it possible for all the people in the populous cities and towns in England to separate on such an occasion as this, and spread themselves over the whole kingdom in smaller numbers, and at proper distances from one another 't is evident even to demonstration, that the plague would have but very little power, and the effects of it be very little felt. For we

PREPARATIONS FOR THE PLAGUE

see evidently that the plague is carried from one to another by infected persons conversing with one another, or by clothes, goods, household stuff or merchandise (which have been infected) being carried from one place to another, and not by any general stagnation of air, or noxious fumes infecting the air, or poisonous particles carried by the winds from one country to another, or from one city to another, as some have imagined.

The effluvia of infected bodies may, and must be indeed, conveyed from one to another by air; so words are conveyed from the mouth of the speaker to the ear of the hearer by the interposition and vibration of the air, and the like of all sounds; but those effluvias cannot extend themselves a great way, but, like ill smells, as they spread they die in the air, or ascend and separate, lose themselves, and are rarefied in the air, so as to lose all their noxious or infectious quality; as the flavour of an orange garden, which in calm weather would be most sensibly felt at a distance all round the trees, will be lost immediately in a high wind, and be only smelt that way which the wind blows.

In the like case, I would caution those people who live in the outparts of, or adjacent places to, infected towns, to observe the blowing of the winds, and if the wind blows from the city towards them, let them for the time keep their windows shut on that side next the said town or city infected, and especially not stand talking or drawing in the air into their mouths that way; but if the wind blows the other way, and blows to the said infected city or town, then

PREPARATIONS FOR THE PLAGUE

they may freely open their windows and doors, and breathe and talk as they will; and this because the stench of the town may be carried some small length on the wings of the wind. But let no man fill the heads of his neighbours with the whimsey of doing this at any considerable distance, such as four or five miles or more, the nature of the thing making it impossible that the poisonous effluvia can keep together so long, or fly so low, as in that part of the air we breathe in, at so great a distance from the place.

If, on the contrary, we pretend by lines and troops to invest or surround any infected place, or a part of the country where such an infected town may lie, I affirm that it is not to be expected that this can be so effectually done as to be certain that none of the people shall get out; and besides the cruelty of locking up so many sound people with the sick, I say, it will never be effectually done.

First of all, for the standing troops, they are not sufficient in number, and 't is supposed the Parliament will hardly consent to raise a new army for such a purpose. As for the militia, how far they may be depended upon for such a service I refer to judgment. The militia are composed of the inhabitants of the neighbouring towns and counties where they serve; it will not be easy to prevent their conniving at the escape of an innocent neighbour, or to prevail upon them to kill a poor honest countryman for endeavouring only to save his own life, or to prevent their taking money to wink and look another way, or to take a wrong aim if they shoot; and,

PREPARATIONS FOR THE PLAGUE

after all, suppose them faithful, it will not be difficult for bold and resolute men, who, being made desperate by the distress they are in, care not for the risk, and are as willing to die one way as another, — I say, it will not be so difficult for twenty or thirty men to join together in the night, and, with arms in their hands, to break through the militiamen, who, 't is known, are not great scholars at the trade of soldiering, when, if they were regular troops, they would not venture it upon any terms.

I shall not enter here upon the debate of the invasion of liberty, and the ruin of property, which must necessarily attend such a practice as this, I mean in case of investing towns. The equity of the case does by no means agree with things done in cases of other extremities, as the blowing up of houses in case of fire, drowning lands in case of an enemy, and the like; but this is really shedding innocent blood, which is a kind of evil not to be done that good may come, no, not of any kind.

More especially I object against this, as it is not likely to answer the means proposed. For example, should an infected person, by any adventure whatever, land at a town on our coast, and, which God of His infinite mercy avert, should he infect the family where he is lodged, shall twenty or thirty thousand people, who perhaps inhabit that town, be immediately surrounded, and, as it were, tied to the infected family till five parts in six of them perish? This was, as I am informed, the case of the city of Toulon, only that the number dead there was exceedingly more; certainly, if on the first surprise the inhabitants had

PREPARATIONS FOR THE PLAGUE

been permitted, or indeed ordered, to retire to some proper place at a distance from the city, and separated as they might have been, the lives of forty thousand people in that town, and the villages near it, had been saved.

It is true that in the time of the last great plague here houses infected were shut up, and it is true that the shutting up of a house is the same thing in its proportion, for that the sound are there shut up with the sick, as it is in a town ; but the case with submission is not the same, for here the sound have time to go away. They may conceal the infected sick person so long, till they that are willing in the family to remove are removed, and then they are not driven back again like murderers, or shot dead for going away.

Besides, in private houses there is some difference in the equity of it, how they are all of a family, and have some obligation upon them to take the risk one with another ; but it is not the same in a whole town, and I cannot but think men have a natural right to flee for the preservation of their lives, especially while they are sound and untainted with the infection ; and 't is a piece of cruelty inconsistent with reason, that because the distemper has reached suppose a house or family at one end of a town, that therefore the families at the other end of the town who are untouched should be imprisoned, and be bound to stay where they are till it comes to them ; and thus, as it were, condemn them to death for that which is their disaster, not their crime, and kill those people for the good of others, of whom the others are in no danger.

PREPARATIONS FOR THE PLAGUE

As for the arguments drawn from necessity and the public safety, 't is fully answered in the proposal above of removing the sound people wholly from the place, and causing them to encamp either in tents or barracks, as the season will permit, till the infection is over.

And this I take to be a much better way (especially where the towns are not too large) than removing the sick immediately into barracks, because the sound can go safely away from the sick, and injure nobody in the remove; whereas the people to be concerned in removing the sick, and the houses they go out of, nay, even the air as they go along, may receive the infection from them, and it may be many ways dangerous to remove them, as well to others as to themselves. But there is no danger of any kind in the sound going away from the sick, except the danger of any infected person going with them, which must be carefully guarded against; and they must remove their camp as often as they find that happen.

It is true this cannot be done in London, or in other considerable cities in general; that is to say, not by all the inhabitants; and there will be always a great number of people who care not to remove, whatever hazard they run. Some, if they should remove, know not whither to go; others have not sufficient to support them if they remove; and others, even though they could remove and have subsistence sufficient, yet will not venture. These we have nothing to say to, neither is there room to say anything of them; what is said above relates only to such as being desirous to remove are not permitted, no,

PREPARATIONS FOR THE PLAGUE

not although they are really sound and free from infection.

Yet there are effectual measures for London and other great cities. For example: *First.* — That upon the approach of the infection, proclamation should be made that all people that intend to remove themselves and families should do it within such a certain time.

Secondly. — All reasonable encouragement should be given to the poorer sort of people who had any friends or relations to receive them, to remove with their families, even to the giving them reasonable allowances for their travelling; that as many poor families as possible may quit the city and separate, which would be their safety, and contribute much to the safety of the whole city also.

Thirdly. — That all such persons as have no legal settlement in the parishes within the city and liberties, &c., should be forthwith passed away by authority and sent home to the parishes from whence they came; no beggars, vagabonds, or loose people to be suffered in the streets.

Fourthly. — All the parish pensioners, alms poor, and poor chargeable upon the parish, as also all the hospital poor, should be immediately removed at the expense of the parishes respectively, to such places as each parish could secure for them, at least twenty miles from London, and to be maintained there at the charge of the public parishes to which they belong.

Fifthly. — All occasion of bringing people to London by the necessity of business should be as much as possible prevented; to which purpose the terms must be adjourned; the Inns of Court shut up; no man should be arrested for debt, so as to be put in prison above a certain time, but that if he could not give bail, or some pledge for his appearance, such debtors should be removed to such public places as the officers of the city should be obliged to prepare, at the distance of fifteen miles at least.

Sixthly. — That all the prisoners for debt should be immediately removed to the same places as above.

Seventhly. — That all criminals, felons, and murderers should be forthwith tried, and such as are not sentenced to die, should be immediately transported or let out on condition of going forty miles from the city, not to return on pain of death.

Eighthly. — That all the children of Christ's Hospital, called the Blue Coat boys and girls, be immediately removed by the government of the said hospital to Hertford and Ware, where they have houses for their reception.

Ninthly. — That all workhouse children, charity children, and all the children of the poor, as are not in condition to maintain them, should be removed into the country, at least thirty miles from the city, and be maintained there by the public.

Tenthly. — That all the masters of families who purpose to abide the extremity be exhorted to send all their children that are under fourteen years of age into the country, and if any of them are destitute of places and friends to send them to, on paying a reasonable sum to the common treasure of the city, care should be taken to provide accommodation for

PREPARATIONS FOR THE PLAGUE

them in the country at the public expense, where they should be well provided for, for a year.

Eleventhly. — That the governors of the Blue Coat Hospital should undertake, on the payment to them of a reasonable sum of money by the city, to provide maintenance for all such children as the city should recommend them, and to be kept in the terms of the hospital, that is to say, as they now keep their other children, not exceeding the number of twenty thousand.

Twelfthly. — That the governors of the workhouses do the like in proportion, so that, in short, all the children in the city and the suburbs should be sent away.

These evacuations of people would greatly lessen the number of the poor in London, and consequently take away the fuel which the fire of the pestilence generally feeds upon.

Thirteenthly. — That after the time first limited for all people that please to remove, if any person after that should desire to remove, he should not be hindered otherwise than on the following conditions : —

1. On bringing good testimony of his body being sound and not infected. This testimony to be given by some able physician or surgeon or other person, after their having searched the person three days successively.

2. On the persons performing a vingtaine, that is to say, a restraint of twenty days, in such barracks or houses as shall be appointed by the magistrates of the city, at some place at least five miles from the suburbs; after which, and no sickness appearing upon him, he shall have testimonials of health, and may go whither he pleases.

PREPARATIONS FOR THE PLAGUE

All these measures being taken at the beginning of the infection, or at the first approach of it, we might reasonably hope, God's infinite mercy concurring, that the city would be in a posture to bear the visitation much better than ever it was before; for though there would be still many thousands of the inhabitants left, yet they would live at large, be unencumbered with poor, and with children, and with all the stench and filth that attend those who want conveniences, and who would in such a calamity only serve to infect one another, and strengthen the contagion in general.

It might be reasonable to suppose that upon this dispersing of the poor people, and sending away the children of all sorts, two-thirds of the inhabitants of London would be absent, including all the families of the better inhabitants, who would voluntarily remove and take country lodgings; of this latter part we might make some guess by what was the case in the last plague in 1665. The removing of the inhabitants was at that time very great, if we may believe the report of those that were then living; I say, it was then very great, for first the whole Court removed to Oxford; there was neither Parliament or term held in London; so that all the nobility and the gentry and lawyers vanished, as it were, at once, and there was scarce a living creature to be seen about the Court. Whitehall was uninhabited, the Park shut up, the passages everywhere stopped; nothing was to be seen at the great houses of the nobility in Westminster and parts adjacent but a servant or two to look after the house, or perhaps nobody within, only a watchman or

PREPARATIONS FOR THE PLAGUE

two at the gate night and day to prevent robbing the house; and as the plague began in St. Giles's parish, the people at that end of the town fled first, so that the streets looked desolate, the grass grew at the doors and upon the steps of the houses, and the streets were in several places barricaded at both ends, the inhabitants being entirely removed and gone. In the city, that is to say, within the walls, as I have been told, about seven thousand houses were quite empty and the doors locked up, and in most of the rest the families were thin, half or more of them gone; and this was without doubt the reason why the number that died in the city was much smaller in proportion than in any other part, there dying more by 4551 in the two parishes of Stepney and Whitechapel than the whole ninety-seven parishes within the walls.

This was doubtless owing to the fewness of the inhabitants within the walls, where the people, being generally wealthy, provided for themselves and their families by an early flight into the country; whereas in the outparts the people lived thicker and closer together, and being poor and wanting conveniences, and not able to flee for want of friends or money, or both, died in heaps, and strengthened the contagion by their numbers.

It is a consideration well worth the concern of the public, how many ways a useful and valuable charity it would be to have the children of the poorer and middling sort of people removed at such a time as that into places of health and air, and to have them taken care of for one year. I cannot think but well-inclined Christians, were it proposed to them, would

PREPARATIONS FOR THE PLAGUE

contribute largely to such a proposal, and what charity and alms would not effect, public stocks should supply. I cannot doubt but a Parliament would consider such a thing, and establish some fund payable by the city, either by a tax on coals, a toll on cattle and corn consumed in the city, or some such thing, upon the security of which money would be easily raised to answer the expense.

By this means the lives of an hundred thousand poor innocent creatures, who, as God was pleased to say of Nineveh, know not their right hand from their left, would be saved, and these children would be preserved for the good of posterity; most of whom would otherwise inevitably perish, some by want, some by neglect, some by the loss of their parents, and the rest by the distemper.

But by this means not a child would be left in the whole city of London, and in all its vast extended suburbs; whereas the distress of poor families in the time of the last plague, by reason of the great numbers of children that lay starving upon their hands, was inexpressible, and the numbers of them that perished in the streets and in empty houses, and in other places full of misery, added exceedingly to the height of the bills of mortality.

When I say an hundred thousand, I do not suggest that there are but an hundred thousand children of fourteen years old and under; I believe there would be found near three times the number within the extent of the bills of mortality; but I suppose one hundred thousand of these to be merely the children of misery and distress, such as must be wholly pro-

PREPARATIONS FOR THE PLAGUE

vided for by charity, and that the rest should be either disposed of by their parents or by the city, that is, by the public, the parents paying a competent sum towards their maintenance, as their ability should appear.

Be it which way it will, I insist upon it that there should not a child be left in the city under fourteen years of age. I could give many reasons why such a step as this would be so necessary for the preserving the health of the city, but I think it will not be disputed.

Having thus cleared all the city of all the poor, and of all the children, and of all the whole family of those who can and will voluntarily flee, I think it will not be needful to say that all other living creatures should be sent away or destroyed, such as dogs, cats, monkeys, parrots, and any creatures that eat flesh, all should be destroyed, whether it be beast or bird, and especially all the weasels, rats and mice, if possible; the first of these, as to dogs and cats, was done in the last visitation, anno 1665, but not the latter.

Also, in my opinion, that there should not be a swine, hog, or sow left alive among the streets or near them, no, nor a horse; not that the horse himself, abstractedly considered, could be dangerous; but as the stables they are kept in, their dung, and the stale or water that comes from them occasion an ill scent, it should be prevented by removing the horses also of all sorts.

Much is said, and great stress is laid by our physicians, upon the article of cleanliness, and removing everything that is nasty and filthy out of the streets, and in consequence of this we find the Grand Juries of London and Middlesex presenting the need there is to put the laws in execution for paving and cleaning the streets, that no noisome, offensive stench may rise from the dirtiness and heaps that are usually found there, especially in the outparts.

I cannot say but there may be something in this; but they that go thus far would do well to go farther and consider those most loathsome by-places, called tide-ditches, which are kept open on the other side of the water, both above bridge and below. They begin from that inlet of water at the Falcon's sluice, spreading every way towards the fields called St. George's Fields, and running through Bandy-Legged Walk, and on the back of the Old Bear Garden up to the Mint. These filthy places receive all the sinks, necessary-houses, and drains from dye-houses, wash-houses, fellmongers, slaughter-houses, and all kinds of offensive trades. They are continually full of carrion, and the most odious of all offensive stench proceeds from them; also the other part of the said ditches westward as far as Lambeth, many of which lie a great depth in mud, and from whence such filthy unsufferable smells are sensibly perceived, as make people loth to pass by them.

The like of these are to be seen below bridge, from Battle Bridge to Horsley Down, and all along the back of Rotherhithe, at least on the hither part of it, and are justly the terror even of the inhabitants themselves.

I could say much on these heads were it needful, and must add that I wonder much that, while the

PREPARATIONS FOR THE PLAGUE

Grand Jury has presented this affair of cleaning and paving the streets, they should omit such notorious fountains of stench, enough to corrupt the very air, and to make people sick and faint as they pass by.

Next to these the hog-keepers' yards at Whitechapel, where swine, which are fed with carrion and the offal of dead beasts, are kept, whose smell is so unsufferably nauseous that people are not able to go that way.

These things would be well worth presenting to the Court of Justice and a Lord Mayor; and I must say that if stinks and nastiness will infect a town, it is owing to nothing but the wonders of God's goodness that this place (Southwark side especially) should be at any time free from infection.

I might here put the inhabitants of this city in mind, and especially the people of Southwark, that in the last great plague the infection held longer in Southwark, in proportion to the place, than in any part of the city or suburbs, and there died more by abundance in that part in proportion to the numbers of people; and this they would do well to consider of upon the occasion now before us; and of the parishes in Southwark, St. Olave's and St. Saviour's which are the particular parishes where the worst of those abominable tide-ditches are buried, more in proportion to their extent than any other of the parishes on that side of the water.

For Example.

From the 19th to the 26th of September the burials stood thus:—

PREPARATIONS FOR THE PLAGUE

St. Saviour's, Southwark	341
St. Olave's, Southwark	324
St. Martin's-in-the-Fields was but	171
St. Giles's-in-the-Fields	107
St. Giles's, Cripplegate	225

From the 26th of September to the 3rd of October:—

St. Saviour's, Southwark	352
St. Olave's, Southwark	278
St. Martin's-in-the-Fields	143
St. Giles's, Cripplegate	196
St. Giles's-in-the-Fields	78

From the 10th to the 17th of October:—

St. Saviour's, Southwark	227
St. Olave's, Southwark	212
St. Martin's-in-the-Fields	60
St. Giles's-in-the-Fields	88
St. Giles's, Cripplegate	43

From the 17th to the 24th of October:—

St. Saviour's, Southwark	101
St. Olave's, Southwark	102
St. Martin's-in-the-Fields	38
St. Giles's-in-the-Fields	38
St. Giles's, Cripplegate	28

In like manner the parishes of Stepney and Whitechapel and Aldgate, where those slaughter-houses and hog-houses are kept, retained the infection longer than any other of the parishes in or about the city of London; much of which (if the skilful physicians may be credited) was owing to those vile places above said.

Another observation of this kind may be made, which will have the like experience to support it, and this is, that it may be observed, that those places of the city itself, as well as of the outparts which lie on the shore or the banks of the river, buried more people in proportion to the extent of their parishes than any other; which may very well be placed to the account of the gullies and common shores, the hog-houses and kennels of the city, which bring all the wash and filth of the streets into the river, under the very noses of the inhabitants; and though it may be true, that the tides do twice a day come up and cover the mouths of the said shores and gullies and carry away the filth, &c., yet when the tide ebbs away it is to be seen what quantities of carrion and nastiness are left above ground, and how nauseous such things are to the inhabitants.

Whether this was the occasion or not, that those parishes butting on the Thames side were more sickly than the rest, I leave to the judgment of all indifferent persons; and especially to those who affirm that these unwholesome smells and unclean, filthy places are a cause and an increase of the infection.

The case is this. In the city, in the parishes following, the burials stood thus for the year 1665:—

St. All-hallows, Barking	514
St. All-hallows the Great	455
St. Andrew by the Wardrobe	476
St. Anne in Blackfriars	652
St. Michael at Queenhith	203
St. Michael, Bassishaw	253

Two of these are only counted large parishes, that is to say, St. All-hallows, Barking, St. Anne, Blackfriars; but all of them buried more in proportion than other parishes of the like magnitude by a great many.

Likewise of the parishes without the walls, as particularly St. Margaret's, Westminster, buried more of the plague than St. Martin's-in-the-Fields by almost a thousand, although the parish of St. Margaret's is not supposed to be half so big as that of St. Martin's.

St. Martin's-in-the-Fields 2183
St. Margaret's, Westminster 3742

The like might be said of other places, but the proportions are not so well known, so I dwell no longer upon that part. I have mentioned these things to show how the opinion of the physicians concerning nastiness and nauseous smells, that they are injurious and dangerous, that they propagate infection, and are a means to increase the plague, is just, and that measures ought to be taken to prevent these things, by keeping the streets clean, well paved, and swept, as the Grand Juries have presented. Adding withal, that the tide-ditches in Southwark, at the Falcon, Lambeth, Rotherhithe, Horsley Down, &c., should be cleansed and kept full of water by proper sluices, to be emptied and let go every spring tide, or else filled up, and not suffered any more. Also that the gullies and common shores running into the Thames on the city side, such as one at St. Catherine's, one at Iron Gate, one near the Custom House, one at Billingsgate, another at Dowgate, and several others, ought to be sunk deeper, arched over, and carried down to low-water mark.

PREPARATIONS FOR THE PLAGUE

But I leave this, as also the managing of Fleet Ditch, and the upper part of it, especially between Holborn Bridge and Hockley-in-the-Hole, a nauseous and abominable sink of public nastiness, — I say, I leave these things to the consideration of the magistrates, who, if they have any regard to the health of the inhabitants, will certainly think that part worth their while to take notice of.

I go on, second, in my own method to such precautions or preparations as are private and personal, and which, I observe, are not much thought of by many people, though I believe the most necessary of all the rest. It is true that the nauseous places which I have mentioned are of dangerous consequence in their kind. But I must say that people ought to turn their thoughts to cleansing a worse jakes than that of the tide-ditches in Southwark or Fleet Ditch, &c., and that is, that the people, especially such as are to stay here at all adventures, should universally cleanse themselves, cleanse their bodies of all scorbutic distempers, ill habits, and especially bad digestures, gross distempers, and the like. It is the doctor's business to tell every man, according to his particular constitution, and according to the temperature of his body and blood, what is fit for him to do. I only here argue the necessity of the thing in general, and touch some general methods, &c.

I know Dr. Mead is not a great friend to evacuations in general, and he says indeed, that he would not have men bring themselves too low, and make too large evacuations, for that it is best to keep the spirit *detailed medical advice (humoural)*

PREPARATIONS FOR THE PLAGUE

in some vigour; and that is good advice where men are in a state of perfect health as 't is called, because Nature ought to be cherished and kept in heart, that she may be able to encounter the great enemy that threatens to invade her.. But the doctor, with submission to his skill, mistakes the case. At the time of the infection I would not by any means have people bring themselves down to sink their spirits by too large evacuations. But taking the case early and by way of preparation, that is to say, six months or more before the infection comes, then it is quite another thing, then there is time to recover the spirits and restore the blood before the time of the distress comes upon them. Then is the time to cleanse the jakes, as I call it — I mean the stomach — and to purge off the foul, corrupted humours collected by long intemperance, luxurious eating, gorging the stomach with sauces and high diet, inflaming the blood with innumerable debauches of wine and the like; I say, now is the time for cleansing the stomach and bowels, and for preparing the body, by delivering Nature from all the burthens she was loaded with before.

Besides, where an ill state of health is the case, though it be not so long before the time, the thing differs extremely, and the man is under a different necessity, for he is concerned to deliver himself from the enemy he has already within him, lest that enemy should confederate with the enemy without, and so the man should be plunged before he is aware.

That the state of our body at the time of the infection renders it more or less susceptible of the infection

PREPARATIONS FOR THE PLAGUE

itself, no man of common-sense will dispute. There is sympathy of parts between the body and the distemper; while the body is clogged, the blood corrupt, the stomach foul, doubtless to receive infected poisonous vapors into the body at that time must put the whole mass of blood into new ferments. We receive poison one of another, and we emit poison one to another; and thus the plague is propagated, though we know not the *modus* in every particular person, for I will not doubt that the infection or distemper is contagious.

If we would be freed from receiving infection, we should certainly assure ourselves that we have no infection already lodged in us; and this must be tried in an effectual manner. The glands of the stomach should be cleansed by frequent emetics, but gentle; the venom of ancient distempers should be purged out of the blood, and therefore gentle salivations would be excellent preparations where they can be allowed of; and let no man object the scandal of that medicine, it is certainly administered in modern practice with great success, in cases not all venereal, and consequently not scandalous. The blood as well as the body must be cleansed, and nothing can so effectually give, as it were, a new and infant blood as this of salivation. And I durst mortgage all my skill in physic, if any one person who being in an ordinary state of health, so as not to be sick of any capital distemper, having taken this a few days, and in but a moderate degree — I say, if any one of these should be afflicted by the plague.

But pray take this with you as you go, that the

PREPARATIONS FOR THE PLAGUE

evacuations or other remedies which I am now speaking of, are not supposed to be so much as thought of after the infection is come, nay, not only after it is come into the body and has touched the spirits, but, I say, not after it is come into the place, for then, when the enemy is at the door, all the forces of Nature are to be mustered together; but all the reinforcements and encouragements that are proper to strengthen Nature for her defence, should be brought to her aid. No garrison ought to have their fortifications to build when the siege against them is laid; all the parts should be done and finished before, and when the siege is laid and the enemy are battering their works, the business then is to counter-batter him, harass him with continual sallies, and be vigilant, ready on all his assaults to repel his forces.

The simile or allusion, I hope, is not improper. Due evacuations as above, and after that temperate and wholesome diet, are the fortifications of Nature, and ought to be the practice of time as long beforehand as possible; but when the enemy is come, then reasonable encouragement ought to be given to the animal spirits, which are the garrison which are to defend the fortress of life; the man must, as it is called, be kept in heart and well supported, that he may not be sunk with apprehensions before it comes, or be surprised with the attack when it comes.

There is another sort of encouragement to prevent these fears and surprises, which I would advise every Christian to prepare and to furnish himself with, and that is the fortifications of the mind. But of that I shall speak by itself.

PREPARATIONS FOR THE PLAGUE

What I say now is, to explain my opinion about purging and cleansing the body by due evacuations, namely, that I particularly limit this to the time we have to prepare against the plague, and that these purgings and cleansings should be done now immediately; that Nature, being delivered in time from all foulness of the stomach, or burthens on the constitution, may be strengthened again, and restored in time, by proper assistance, for the combat with her great enemy.

All sinks and receptacles of filthiness, say the doctors, must be cleansed for the preserving our health by sweetening the air we breathe in; but what a sink and receptacle of filth is the body of man? How is he to be restored but by cleansing and purging off the noxious slime and corroded juices which are dispersed in all the vessels of the body, even those vessels which common cathartics will not reach?

It is upon this account that I propose to as many as have courage for such a medicine the use of a gentle salivation.

The mercury is represented to be a strainer to the blood, which takes all the phlegmatic and corrupted parts away from it, giving a change to the whole mass of blood, and consequently giving a new constitution to the body; the man lays, or has laid in him, new principles of life, and these are not by far so subject to infection as other bodies are.

They who do not think fit to do this must run more risk than other people, and how can such promise themselves safety when an infection comes? Who can think himself safe in a magazine of powder

PREPARATIONS FOR THE PLAGUE

with a candle in his hand? If men will meet an infection with gross and foul bodies, corrupted with the nauseous fumes of ill-digested meats, with a blood inflamed with excess and intemperance, whether of one sort or another, and will not apply themselves to such remedies for recovering the rectitude of their constitutions as reason and physic direct, such men may as well follow the practice of the Turks, who, upon principles of predestination, visit their friends when the plague is upon them, go promiscuously and unconcerned one among another upon their ordinary occasions, without so much as inquiring whether the plague be among them or not, or declining them when they know it is.

But if we believe the plague is received by contagion, and that means may be made use of to prevent it, we ought to use those means which are proper, and use them in the time that is proper too; otherwise we may as well omit the means wholly, and leave all to Nature and Providence.

I might enter here upon an easy proof, that our ordinary way of living in England requires the evacuations more than is the case of the people of other nations, and that if the infection should come among us, which I pray God to prevent, it will find much more fuel to feed on than it does in other countries where people live more temperately, and where they feed cleaner than we do here.

We saw plainly the difference in this matter in the late great plague in Sweden and Denmark, where the malignity of the distemper was far less than in England in 1665; and even in the plague in 1665

PREPARATIONS FOR THE PLAGUE

we found our people in the south parts, where we live more plentifully and feed more grossly, were much more violently infected than in Scotland or in the north of England, even in proportion to the numbers.

Next, therefore, to medicines for the carrying off the fund of distemper which is to be found in us, and which we owe to the irregular diet and intemperance of our people, I must recommend to all people to alter their manner of life, to eat, but especially to drink, more moderately, and, in a word, to live temperately and sparing; to eat less flesh, less sauce, and less of the half-digested juices and gravy of their meats, which a most pernicious custom has inured them to, by which they are brought to eat their meat half roasted and half boiled.

It is a most unaccountable habit that we are brought to by our vitiated appetites in this nation, namely, to eat our flesh meat, of which also we feed immoderately, almost raw; indeed, some people may be said to feed little different from the Tartars, who eat their horse-flesh raw. If we were but to be seen by the people of any other country how we eat, especially our wild fowl, the flesh scarce warm through, and all the undigested impurities of the entrails and inside of them serving for our sauce, — I say, when strangers see us feeding thus, they must be allowed to take us, as they do, to be, if not cannibals, yet a sort of people that have a canine appetite; and it was the modestest thing I could expect of them, when in foreign countries I have heard them describe our way of feeding in England, and tell us that we devour

our meat, but do not eat it, viz., devour it as the beasts of prey do their meat with the blood running between their teeth.

Let no man flatter himself in his feeding in this gross manner; the body so fed is prepared not against, but for, a contagion, and we have much reason to fear that if we should now be visited, such a visitation will find us half prepared for it to work upon, and consequently we shall receive the distemper with more danger.

Some people tell us of the plague being propagated by insects, and these carried from place to place in the air in an unaccountable manner, which if it were true, one place would be apparently infected as well as any other, and at the same time, as blights in our orchards frequently run over the whole kingdom. I leave those philosophers to be confuted by the physicians, who have much better and more rational accounts to give of the beginning, propagating, and spreading the infection. But that foul bodies and gross feeding make us more receptible of infection than we should otherwise be, this seems to be a truth that both sides must grant.

Temperate diet, and avoiding excesses in strong drink, which so many ways debauch not the head only but even the whole constitution, should be avoided as carefully before the plague; I say, as carefully as we should avoid conversing with an infected body in the time of the plague.

If I can give any credit to the assurances of those who lived in London in the time of the last great plague, few of those people we call drunken sots

PREPARATIONS FOR THE PLAGUE

escaped the distemper. It is an odd way of observing on such things, and therefore I desire to explain myself. By the words drunken sot, I mean a sort of people who have by a habit of drinking to excess brought themselves to sottism, that have debilitated themselves, their bodies as well as their understandings, and are come to dozing over their drink; who make their drink their food, eat little, and sip to keep their spirits up. I need not describe what I mean by a sot; but, according to my friends' relation, these men all went off; some that drank hard, but had strong constitutions and that were not conquered by their drink, though they were often drunk, outlived it, and had not the distemper; but the others were generally carried off.

What I infer from this is, that intemperance in drinking, as it is destructive to the constitution, so it is a most dreadful induction to the plague. When the spirits are attacked by the venom of the infection, they, being already exhausted, are in no condition to defend the body, and so the man dies, of course.

We make a great stir, as I have said, about avoiding smells in time of infection, and one[1] tells us, weakly enough, that the city of London was so close built in the time of the plague in 1665, that the air had not a free course sufficient to purify the streets, also that the streets were not paved, &c., which, 't is insinuated, added to the ill smells which propagated the distemper; both which as they are but trifling in themselves, so they are really false in fact; for the

[1] Bradley, in his book called "The Plague of Marseilles Considered."

PREPARATIONS FOR THE PLAGUE

streets of London were paved then as well as now, and the streets that were then may be judged by the breadth and buildings of those streets which remain still, where the fire did not come, and which, though they were not quite so open and wide as the new buildings are, yet are they far from being so close as to affect the health of the city. Besides, the weakness of his inference is evident another way, viz., it is apparent that the greatest rage of the infection at the time was in the outparts, where the buildings were the same as they are now, as in the parishes of St. Giles-in-the-Fields, St. Martin-in-the-Fields, St. Andrew, Holborn, &c., on the west part of the town; and in the parishes of Cripplegate, Bishopsgate, Aldgate, Whitechapel, Stepney, &c., on the east and north, in all which parts the neighbourhood of the fields prevented all interruption of air; whereas in the close-built city, as he calls it, they were healthier than in any other part.

Dr. Mead, likewise, opposes his private opinion against the common experience of the town in the late plague, 1665, and against the advice of all the physicians that were then in practice, about keeping fires in the houses and streets at that time, which was used with very good success; and it was found by experience that those people who kept fires night and day in their houses, were much freer than others from infection, the heat of the fire rarefying the air, and dissipating, if not consuming, the infectious vapours or particles, call them which we will, with which the air on such occasions is supposed to be filled.

PREPARATIONS FOR THE PLAGUE

It was on this account that the citizens, by order of the Lord Mayor, and the Lord Mayor by advice of the College of Physicians, kept great fires night and day at the corner of the streets, at the gate of the Exchange, and in other public places; by which they believed, at least, the passing and repassing the principal streets of the city, where the greatest numbers of people came, was kept wholesome, or at least more wholesome than other places.

The great quantity of coals burnt in public and in private on that occasion may confute that foolish assertion of the author above mentioned first, viz., that at the same time sea coal was hardly in use. I think I need say no more of that ridiculous part than to quote a paragraph out of his book, every branch of which is contradicted by the knowledge and experience of thousands now living. His words are as follows, viz.:—

"London, at the time of the plague, 1665, was perhaps as much crowded with people as I suppose Marseilles to have been when the plague began. The streets of London were in the time of the pestilence very narrow, and, as I am informed, unpaved for the most part; the houses by continued jetts one storey above another, made them almost meet at the garrets, so that the air within the streets was pent up, and had not due freedom of passage to purify itself as it ought. The food of the people was then much less invigorating than in these days. Foreign drugs were but little in use, and even Canary wine was the highest cordial the people would venture upon, for brandy, some spices, and hot spirituous liquors were then not in fashion;

PREPARATIONS FOR THE PLAGUE

and at the time sea coal was hardly in use, but their firing was of wood, and for the most part chestnut, which was then the chief furniture of the woods about London, and in such quantity, that the greatest efforts were made by the proprietors to prevent the importation of Newcastle coal, which they represented as an unwholesome firing, but, I suppose, principally because it would hinder the sale of their wood; for the generality of men were, I imagine, as they are now, more for their own benefit than for the common good.

"The year 1665 was the last that we can say the plague raged in London, which might happen from the destruction of the city by fire the following year 1666, and besides the destroying the eggs, or seeds, of those poisonous animals that were then in the stagnant air, might likewise purify that air in such a manner as to make it unfit for the nourishment of others of the same kind which were swimming or driving in the circumambient air. And again, the care that was taken to enlarge the streets at their rebuilding, and the keeping them clean after they were rebuilt, might greatly contribute to preserve the town from pestilence ever since."

Nothing can be more contrary to experience and the truth of fact than this whole story together or apart. (1) To say London was supplied with wood for fuel in the year 1665, and that coal was hardly in use: whereas in very little while after we found the Parliament thought 1s. 6d. per chaldron upon coals a sufficient tax for the rebuilding St. Paul's Cathedral, and all the churches that were lost by the

PREPARATIONS FOR THE PLAGUE

fire; and I appeal to the coal-meters' book, which were then set up, for the quantity of coals then consumed in London and the parts adjacent.

Then that the woods about London were chiefly of chestnut. That they were so about 300 years before, I believe may be true; but as the oldest man alive cannot remember one wood of chestnut standing near London, or so much as a chestnut tree left among all the woods near London, it is strange this gentleman should take upon him to write that which so many people now alive can contradict.

Again, as to the wines which people then drank, this gentleman is most ridiculously mistaken; for when he gives the want of the use of brandy and hot spirituous liquors as for a proof that the plague increased upon them, their diet not being so invigorating as now; on the contrary, I insist that the food of the people was rather more invigorating than it is now. For as this gentleman chiefly mentions the wines they drank, I oppose to it, and appeal to the knowledge of the whole town, that if they had not so great a variety of wines to drink, they had no adulterated wines to poison and debauch their blood as we have.

If Canary was their highest cordial, I must tell him that they had then only the best, most generous, and most sanitive wine in the world for their cordial, and well it were if we, their self-wise posterity, had such cordials as they had; that is to say, that our Canary was only our cordials, and that our other wines were not adulterated and poisoned as they are; and especially considering that we do not drink wine

PREPARATIONS FOR THE PLAGUE

now by drams, that is to say, by small quantities, and as cordials, as they did, but by quarts and gallons, that we make our physic our food, and drink diseases upon ourselves which our ancestors at the late plague knew nothing of.

In like manner 't is a mistake to say that they had no brandy or cordials at that time; the Custom House books abundantly contradict it, and it is too recent in our memory for any man of years to forget, that the people had their aqua vitæ and other distilled waters to drink as cordials on all occasions that required cordials.

But it is true that there was not two thousand brandy-shops and twelve hundred punch-houses in London, as they say there are now; and that the spirits which are now distilled (or rather half-drawn) from malt and musty grounds, are rather adapted to poison and destroy mankind than to be cordials to their blood.

It is out of the question that the people of England lived more regular, and, if I may judge of it, fared better in those days by far, than they do now. What they ate and drank then was much more invigorating than our way of living now is; for this gentleman, though a member of the Royal Society, must not tell us that intemperance is an invigorating way of living: drinking wine as we drink wine, corrupted, adulterated, and poisoned; drinking punch by gallons made of malt spirits, stinking, as I may justly call it, of the humid, and half-drawn from the half-brewed worts. Could any man of common-sense instance the temperate living of those days as a reason why the plague spread with more violence, and then bring up the drunken sordid swallowing down foul liquors, and gorging ourselves with poison and stench, as a reason why we should bear it off better than they?

On the contrary, I must insist that our vices, which are already a plague upon our morals, are a dreadful kind of fuel for a contagion, and miserably prepare us for a plague upon our bodies. As to the havoc they make of conscience and religion, and the ruin they are to souls, I refer that to its place.

Our forefathers had sins enough, no doubt, and for which Heaven brought judgment upon them most righteously; but our forefathers never were guilty of the luxury that we practise, neither in kind or in degree.

But besides this, the author I am speaking of should have gone a little farther back, too, for the deficiency in good liquors which he mentions, than the year, '65; for the flux of wine from France, which began to supply us, and the breach made on people's morals by excesses, were really begun some time before, namely, at the restoration of civil peace, and the people were arrived to some degrees of proficiency in debauchery by that time, though not to the violent height which they are come to since.

I bring it home to our present case thus: If the plague made such progress in those days, when people lived in a so much more temperate manner than they do now, how much more reason have we to apprehend its progress now, when the bodies of men are debauched with excesses in meats and drinks, and all kinds of intemperance? From the whole, it is highly to the purpose to press our people to use proper remedies, to clean their bodies of all the gross exhalations and nauseous humours which fly up to the brain from a foul stomach, and from corrupted juices in the body; and to show how much reason there is to change our way of living, and begin a temperate course of diet, that Nature, after having had the assistance of medicine, may be invigorated and supported for the combat she is to enter into.

I persuade myself that what I have said here is so just, and is supported by such reason, as it will not be disputed. I cannot but think that if these things were effectually considered and put in practice, the people of this city would fare much better for it in a time of infection; and I am sure they would have particular satisfaction in the experiment.

FAMILY PREPARATIONS AGAINST THE PLAGUE

I include these preparations under the head of private, as opposed to the public preparations I spoke of in the first general; but they are a kind of public, as they are different from the preparations last mentioned, which are personal and particular.

I must for the sake of this head suppose that the plague (God forbid it) was at the door, or perhaps really begun in the nation. Next to the physicking the body, as I have said, and entering into a regular and temperate life, it comes to be considered, how families are to manage themselves, and in what manner of posture people should propose to put themselves, if possible to prevent the contagion breaking in upon them.

The pestilence being, as has been said, a contagious distemper, it is one of the first principles in the argument now in hand, that every family should keep themselves from conversing with one another, that is to say, from conversing with the streets as much as possible.

When a house is infected with the plague, we shut it up; this was done in the late plague, 1665, with great severity; the design is to keep the common people from conversing with the infected families. When a house is sound and uninfected, they should shut themselves up, to keep them from conversing with the common people, who perhaps may be infected. The first is done to keep the families from giving the plague to the common people; the last should be done to keep the common people from giving the plague to the family; and the reasons are a just alternative. Nature dictates the one as well as the other; and let the inconveniences be what they will, it is certain the thing is so necessary, and the success so visible and promising, that no family can repent the design of doing it; many have repented sorely that they did not do it, or did not do it in time.

'T is no new thing to direct people to live as retired in their houses as possible in time of infection; but the case is, that people will not confine themselves, or will not put themselves in a condition to do it effectually, and I must add, that not to do it effectually, that is strictly, is not to do it at all. Nay,

PREPARATIONS FOR THE PLAGUE

not to do it strictly, is worse than not to do it at all, as I shall show presently.

I know a family at this time living in Marseilles, who having effectually locked themselves up within their own house, and never conversed with the people of the town, never had the distemper at all; and yet Marseilles, if we may believe the accounts we have seen from thence, was in a far more violent manner infected than ever the city of London was.

If we may believe the accounts from Provence, there died in Marseilles, and the villages within a league of it, above 60,000 people.

If we may believe the bills of mortality published in the city of London for the year 1665, there died of the plague in London, and the villages about it, that is to say, within the lines of communication, 68,596 in that year, and no more.

Now, all people that know the two cities of London and Marseilles, will acknowledge there is no comparison in the dimensions, or in the number of inhabitants, between the one and the other. If there died 60,000 people in Marseilles, it will be granted that there died at least two-thirds of the people; for they who reckon 90,000 people to have been in that city for the usual number of inhabitants, are, in my opinion, sure to reckon enough. Should the plague, then, of 1665 have swept away in London a proportion to what it did in Marseilles, there must have died even then above 400,000 people, which would have been a dreadful time indeed.

Again, the case in London was really moderate, compared to that of Marseilles; for though, it is

PREPARATIONS FOR THE PLAGUE

true, there were few people seen in the streets of London in the height of the infection, yet, on the other hand, the dead bodies did not lie unburied in the streets in heaps; the sick were not laid out in blankets and on couches in the streets, to expire in the open air; the poisoned bedclothes and furniture in which the infected had lived, and on which the miserable wretches had given up the ghost, were not to be seen in London lying out in the streets and at the doors, to be trampled on as the people went along; all which was the case at Marseilles; so that if the particles of infection were in the air, as some people suggest, it was next to impossible to escape it there.

Now, if the family I speak of did escape the infection in such a place as Marseilles, and in such a time, and next under God's providence by the circumspection they used with regard to conversing with others, much more might it be so in the city of London, whatever may happen, if the distemper be not so violent as to despise all precaution, and to infect people that never come abroad.

It is true, for a family in London to live perfectly retired in the time of a visitation is scarce practicable; nay, unless they are sufficiently stored with provisions of all sorts for their subsistence, with physic, clothes, and all other necessaries, it is not possible; and for want of this, as well at Marseilles as at London, many thousands of families were infected who might otherwise have been preserved.

In order to direct any particular family who have substance to enable them to shut themselves up in so strict a manner as would be absolutely necessary for preserving them effectually from contagion to be received from any other person, or the goods or clothes of any that are infected, I shall here describe a family shut up, with the precautions they used, how they maintained an absolute retreat from the world, and how far they provided for it, it being partly historical and partly for direction; by which pattern, if any family upon the like occasion thinks fit to act, they may, I doubt not, with the concurrence of Providence, hope to be preserved.

The family I speak of lived in the parish of St. Alban's, Wood Street. They consisted of the master of the family and his wife, being either of them between forty and fifty years of age, the man about eight-and-forty, the wife about two-and-forty, and in pretty good state of health. There were five children, three daughters and two sons, two maid-servants and an apprentice; the person was a considerable dealer, and by trade a wholesale grocer. He had another apprentice near out of his time, a porter, and a boy, who he kept all employed in his business; but, seeing the desolation that was coming upon the city, he dismissed the boy, gave him sufficient to carry him to his friends in Staffordshire, and made him go away directly with the carrier. His eldest apprentice he gave the remainder of his time to, and he went away likewise by consent. As to the porter, he did not lodge in his house before, so there was no occasion of dismissing him; but, being a poor man, and likely to fall into distress for want of his employ, he obliged him to come every day,

PREPARATIONS FOR THE PLAGUE

and sit at the door from nine in the morning to six at night as a watchman, and to receive any orders, go of necessary errands, carry letters to and from the post-house, and the like; and had a wicket made in the door, to take in or give out anything they thought fit; besides which there was a rope fastened to a little pulley to draw up anything from the streets, or let anything down. By this rope they often let down victuals and cordials, and what else they thought fit, to this poor man the porter, and especially his wages constantly every week, or oftener as he wanted it.

The master having resolved thus to shut himself up and all his family, he first took measures for storing himself with all manner of provisions for his house, so that, if possible, he might not be under a necessity to send for anything out of doors, resolving to make it a standing rule that the door should not be opened on any account whatever; that the dearest friend he had in the world should not come into him, nor the greatest necessity in the world, fire excepted, oblige any one of his house to go out of the doors into the streets; nor would he suffer any of his family so much as to look out of a window into the street, or open any casement, except a wooden window made for the purpose, where the pulley and rope was, and that up two pair of stairs; and this wooden window he caused to be covered with thin plates of latin, or tin, that nothing infected or infectious should stick to it.

Whenever this wooden window was opened, he caused a flash of gunpowder to be made in the room, so as to fill it with smoke, which, as soon as the window was opened, would gush out with some force, so that it carried away what air was at the window, not suffering any to come in from abroad, till it was purified and sufficiently singed with the sulphur that goes with the gunpowder smoke.

While this smoke lasted, he that looked out of the window talked with the porter at the gate, let down to him or drew up from him what he had occasion for; but if the smoke of the gunpowder abated, he immediately shut the door till he had made another flash with powder within.

Before the time of shutting himself and family in, and as soon as he found there would be a necessity of it, he carefully furnished himself with stores of all sorts of provisions, but did it privately, and with as little noise as he could; and his magazine was as follows: First, as he was ten in family, he allowed them to eat a pound of bread each per day; but as he laid in a quantity of meal besides, he abated one sixth part for cake bread, and such other sorts as might be made in the house; so he bought three thousand pound weight of biscuit bread such as is baked for ships going to sea, and had it put up in hogsheads, as if going to be shipped off, so that the biscuit baker knew nothing but that it was for a ship that he was fitting out. Then he caused it to be taken away in a boat, and bringing it up to Queenshithe, landed it there, and carried it by cart into his warehouse, as if it had been hogsheads of grocery.

In like manner he caused twenty barrels of fine flour to be bought and packed up, as they pack up

PREPARATIONS FOR THE PLAGUE

fine flour for Barbadoes or Jamaica. I mention this because it is known that unless flour be thus packed up and pressed with great art together in a cask, and then headed close up, so that no air can get to it, it will spoil, be musty, breed the weevil, and corrupt.

Then he caused a small oven to be built on the top of his house, that is to say, in a chimney in one of his garrets, for fear, and laid in as many faggots for the heating it as would serve to heat it three times in two weeks for a whole year.

He then bought twelve hogsheads of good middling beer, which he had caused to be brewed on purpose for keeping, being so well hopped that there was no doubt of its being sound; and having a good vault for keeping them, they were stowed by themselves; and that those might be supposed to supply him fully, he had six half hogsheads of other beer laid in for present use.

He took care for a reasonable quantity of wine, cordial waters, and brandy, not for mirth or plentiful drinking, but for necessary supplies, the physicians also having advised every one that could afford it to drink moderately, so as not to suffer their spirits to sink or be dejected, as on such melancholy occasions they might be supposed to do.

To this end he bought a half hogshead of the best Canary wine that he could get in the whole city.

Two small casks of Malmsey, quantity about twelve gallons each.

One quarter cask of Malaga sack.

One small runlet of tent or muscadine.

PREPARATIONS FOR THE PLAGUE

Two small runlets of aqua vitæ.

Twelve gallons of aniseed water.

Two runlets of eight gallons each of brandy, which was then very rare.

His wife and daughters had stored their closets well with many sorts of distilled waters, as well simple waters as others, and particularly a new cordial prepared by a prescription of the physicians at that time, and called plague water; of this, though very costly, they had prepared the quantity of two dozen bottles.

Also his wife and two eldest daughters had stored their closet with several preparations of medicines, as directed by the physicians, as mithridate, Venice treacle, diascordium, and pill. ruff., London treacle, diachylon, turpentine, &c.

Also they collected all needful sorts of herbs and roots, such as rue, mint, wormwood, carduus, angelica, garlic, scabius, white lily roots, sage, sorrel, and other useful simples, which they kept dry, to use by the prescriptions of medicine published by the College; so that they might make up these things, if need was, without the help of an apothecary or surgeon.

But to return to provisions. The master of the house, like a prudent purveyor, took care to do everything without clamour or noise, so that he might not be known to lay in a great store of provisions; the danger of such things being made public being often great, and no doubt would have been so, had the city suffered any scarcity of provisions, which, however, by the prudence of the magistrates, was prevented; but, as that was more than he knew would happen, he laid in all his provisions with the utmost privacy.

Having furnished himself with bread, with flour, and with beer, in the next place he went to a butcher in Rotherhithe, none having yet died of the plague on that side of the water, and here he caused three fat bullocks to be killed, and the flesh pickled and barrelled up, as if done for a ship going on a long voyage; likewise six barrels of pork for the same pretended occasion. These also he brought by water to Trigg Stairs, where he landed them and carted them to his warehouse as before, as if it had been grocery.

He then wrote to several correspondents he had in the country, and caused twenty flitches of bacon to be sent him, some from one place, some from another, so that they did not come to him all together, nor above two or three from any particular carrier.

He likewise had a large stock of cheeses, particularly out of Wiltshire and Warwickshire and Gloucestershire, about six hundredweight in the whole. He bought also five very large old Cheshire cheeses, so that he had a store of cheese for much more than a year.

Out of Suffolk, he had sent him twelve firkins of the best salt butter that could be had; besides that he had several pots of butter sent him by particular order from other countries where he had dealings.

He took particular care to lay in about a ton and a half of good white wine vinegar, as a thing that

PREPARATIONS FOR THE PLAGUE

was particularly useful on many occasions. He laid in a double or threefold stock of coals and wood for firing, with gunpowder and brimstone for scents above; also salt and pickles in abundance, being judged very wholesome, with some hams, neats' tongues, and hung beef for dainties; with about twenty small jars or stone bottles of good oil, rather for physical uses than for salads, for these they were sure to be without.

Thus you have, as near as I can collect, his bill of stores, and the magazine was certainly well filled.

It is true every family could not do thus; but 't is also true that if all those that could have done so had done it, and had done it in time, the contagion had not spread as it did in so many substantial families; for though it was said, which, however, I do not grant, that none of the market people were infected who carried provisions to supply the city, yet this I can undertake to say, and could prove it by many people still living, that abundance of people got the distemper by going to market to buy those provisions, that is to say, by going out into the street to fetch such necessaries as they wanted, whether at shops or in the markets; and therefore it was the most necessary precaution that could be taken by this or any other person, to lay in a fund of provisions for his whole family, so as not to be obliged to have any person go out of his house into the street, by which he was as much separated from the people of the city as if he had lived several miles off from them.

I should have mentioned that he took care to have

PREPARATIONS FOR THE PLAGUE

all other needful petty things provided, such as shoes, hose, gloves, and all sorts of linen and wearing clothes, so that nothing could be wanted that they need go out for of that kind.

→ Does anyone care?

As to spice and fruit, and all such things, they had sufficient in the house by the means of their trade as a grocer; and as to perfumes of many kinds, he provided a great quantity.

Candles he laid in about seventy or eighty dozen, that is to say, dozen pound, with a great many bottles of lemon juice and lime juice, those acids being very necessary on that occasion. He doubly stored the house also with vessels of all sorts, such as earthenware, glass-ware, and all such perishable things.

He caused all the rats and mice in his house to be effectually poisoned and destroyed, and all the cats and dogs to be killed, and buried deep in the ground in his yard.

He built up three great terrace cisterns, and had them kept constantly filled with water, that every room in his house might be frequently washed; and not content with water of the New River in his yard, which came in by a pipe, he caused a well to be sunk in his said yard and a pump placed there, that he might have water to dress their provisions with, which did not run open in the city air, or that could be touched with any dead carcass, or have any living body or clothes washed in it which were infected with the plague.

His last and greatest concern was for fresh meat, and this he could not contrive any way for, and therefore, excepting that he made some provisions of live fowls, which he caused to be kept for the sake of having a few eggs in the house, and for now and then a fowl to eat, he resolved to be content without either mutton, lamb, or veal, and this was the greatest mortification they suffered as to provisions.

With these preparations he began. He forbore shutting himself quite in for several months after the plague was begun, and even till there died above 1000 a week; because that, though the infection was very terrible in the out-parishes, and especially in the west part of the town, that is to say, in Holborn, St. Giles, Fleet Street, and the Strand, yet the city was very healthy, nor was the distemper felt within the walls to any degree till the latter end of June or the beginning of July; for in the second week of July, when there died, as by the weekly bills appeared, 1268 of all distempers, yet there died but twenty-eight of the plague in all the ninety-seven parishes within the walls, and but sixteen in the whole body of buildings on the Surrey side of the water.

However, the next week after it was doubled again; and, as he foresaw the infection o'erspreading the whole city and all the outparts like a dreadful torrent, as he had always said it would do, he begun to put his resolutions more strictly in execution; for from the beginning of July he suffered none of his family to stir out without the walls of the city, nor in the city to any public place, market, exchange, church, or the like, and wrote to all his dealers and correspondents in the country not to write for any more goods, for that he could not send anything out

PREPARATIONS FOR THE PLAGUE

into the streets to the carriers or receive anything in from them.

The 1st of July he began to place his porter without the door, where he built him a little hutch to sit in, and where he (the porter) received all messages and errands, and delivered them as he got admittance at a wicket in the door, and gave such answers again when called for as he was directed. By the 14th of July the plague was increased in a dreadful manner in the outparts, so that the bills amounted that week to 1762 of all distempers, 1500 of which might be supposed to die of the plague, and the number still increasing, their own parish being the second that was infected in the city. I say, on the 14th of July he shut the wicket of his door up, and bolted, barred, and locked himself in with all his house, taking the keys into his own keeping, declaring to all his family that if any one of them, though it was his eldest son and daughter, should offer to stir out without the door, though it was but a yard off, they should not come in again upon any terms whatever.

At the same time he nailed up all the casements of his windows, or fastened the wooden shutters on the inside.

N.B. — They had no sash windows in those days, nor for many years after.

This he did because it had been the opinion of some physicians that there were at least many unwholesome steams and infectious smells in the air, especially in those close streets and among the houses where the plague was already spread; and it was

[57]

more than ordinarily observed by curious people that in the houses which were infected, and had been shut up, and where several persons, or perhaps the whole family, had died, there was a strange clammy or dewy sweat on the inside of the glass of the window, like the sweat that will be on the windows in a damp morning; [and] that this did not melt off with the heat of the sun as in other cases, but rather consisted the stronger. That this was the poisonous air breathed out of the infected people's bodies who had died of the plague was not doubted; but whether this was infectious in its nature, and would, if the windows had been opened, have infected the next houses, or the next people that had sucked it in with their breath, this, I say, was not determined, neither do I determine it, though to me it seems reasonable that it should do so. However, this prudent householder, acting also by the direction of good physicians, closed up all his windows as above, except the wooden shutter kept open for conversing with his porter without doors, as above; he also made chimney boards to close up all those chimneys in which he did not keep constant fires, as I shall observe afterwards.

Till this time he had taken fresh meat of a country woman, a higgler, who assuring him she brought it from Waltham Abbey Market, and opened it not till she came to his door, he had some satisfaction on it; but now he forbid her also, and allowed her coming no more.

Now, therefore, he opened his magazine, and distributed bread by weight to his family. It was long

PREPARATIONS FOR THE PLAGUE

ere his children could be brought to eat the coarse and hard sea-biscuit bread, and he was fain to distribute to them more meal and fine flour than he purposed at first, and they made themselves cakes and small loaves of bread as they could; but in a little time they were used to the other, and they found ways to soak and soften them by such mixtures as they could get.

Being now entirely shut up, they scarce knew how it fared with their neighbours, except that they heard the knells continually sounding; and their porter gave them in weekly bills of mortality, where they might see what dreadful havoc the infection made in the town round about them.

After they had been shut up about three weeks, their porter gave them an account that the next house to them but two was infected; that three houses on the other side of the way were shut up, and that two servants, out of another house on the same side of the way but on the other side of their house, were sent away to the pest house beyond Old Street.

It was observable that it went hardest with the poor servants of such families, because of their being often obliged to go out on errands to fetch things which the family wanted to which they belonged; as particularly to the markets and to the apothecaries' and chandlers' shops, which latter were at that time the principal market for all necessaries, except in flesh meat, fish, &c.

It was a great satisfaction to them that the people in the next house to them on one side were all gone

PREPARATIONS FOR THE PLAGUE

away into the country at the beginning of the visitation, and had left the house all locked up, all the windows barred on the inside, and boarded up on the outside, and had left the charge of the house with the constable and watch.

The next houses to them on the other side were all inhabited and visited, and at length all shut up, and in one or more of them the whole families perished.

By this time they heard a bell go ringing nightly along the streets, but they knew not what it meant, it not being like the sound of the ordinary bellman; and though they heard a voice with the bell, yet as it did not go at first by their door, so they could not distinguish what it was they said; and as their porter did not sit at their door in the night as he did in the day, they could not inquire; but at length their porter informed them that the number of people that died was so great in the outparts that it was impossible to bury them in form, or to provide coffins for them, nobody daring to come into the infected houses; and that therefore the Lord Mayor and Aldermen had ordered carts to go about with a bellman to carry away the dead bodies; that this had been done in the parishes of Holborn and St. Sepulchre, Cripplegate, and other large parishes, above a fortnight, and that they began now to come into the city, and that in particular to the parish of St. Olave, Silver Street, which was very sickly, and that the carts were come thither the night before.

This was frightful enough, Silver Street being also

the next parish to St. Alban's, only on the other side of the way, and the distemper raged violently in both, so that during that fortnight, which was the middle of August, there died near fourscore in those two small parishes, and still increasing. The reason of this might be partly the joining of both the parishes to the Cripplegate side of the wall, and the parish of Cripplegate was at that time dreadfully visited, the plague being come down that way from St. Giles-in-the-Fields, where it began; and the weight of the infection during the latter end of August and the beginning of September lay chiefly on that side of the city, from whence it went on to Bishopsgate, and Shoreditch, and Whitechapel, and so to Stepney, taking the city with it, which was, as it were, carried down with the stream; for the infection came, as we may say, first into the city at Cripplegate, and so spread in a few weeks quite over it.

At this time, viz., from the beginning to the end of August, or the end of the first week in September, there died from 700 to 800, and almost 900 a week in Cripplegate parish only, and then it was that the carts were employed in that parish. It was indeed impossible to bury so many in the ordinary way, for there died 4000 people in five weeks' time in that parish, so that neither could coffins be made or graves dug for them, or even churchyards be found to lay them in; so that they were fain to obtain a grant of a piece of land from the city in Finsbury Fields adjoining to the Artillery grounds, which was given them for a burying-ground, and remains so to this day, in which they dug vast pits, and threw the

PREPARATIONS FOR THE PLAGUE

bodies into them nightly by cartloads, always covering those with earth in the morning who were thrown in overnight, and then next night throwing in more bodies and more earth, and so on till the pit was filled, so that, as it was reported by the parish officers, about 2200 people were thrown into one of those pits. But this is a digression.

All this while the family continued in health, and the cheerful parent encouraged them to hope for preservation, whatever might happen without doors; but when he had such bad news every day from without doors, and that every night he heard the dismal bell with the cart, and the voice following it in a mournful tone, "Bring out your dead, bring out your dead," it could not but make heavy impressions upon the minds of the master and mistress of the family, and they began to look upon one another with sad hearts, believing they were all but dead corpses, and that the visitation was so appointed by Heaven as that it would sweep away the whole body of the inhabitants, and that none would be left alive.

In this distress he prudently ordered all his family to lodge on the lower floor, that is to say, up one pair of stairs, and as many of them to lie single as possible, and had all the rooms above furnished with beds to lay any of the family in that should be taken sick; so that if any were taken sick they were to be immediately removed into some of those upper rooms, as to an infirmary, where they should be separated entirely from the rest of the family, and a nurse procured from abroad to tend them, and to be drawn up by the pulley to the wooden shutter, so as not to

PREPARATIONS FOR THE PLAGUE

come through the house at all or converse with any in the family.

In ordering this, he appointed that if he himself should be taken, he would go immediately into the infirmary and be attended by a nurse as above; and that none of his children should be suffered to come up the stairs, or come near him; and that if he should die, his body should be let down by the pulley also into the cart, &c., and so of the whole house. Though his wife assured him that if he was taken ill she would go up into the infirmary and be shut up with him.

We must suppose this gentleman to have more prudence than religion, and much more care of his body than of his soul, and so of the rest of his family, if he took no care all this while of his house as to their worshipping God; be pleased, therefore, to suppose, that as he was a serious, pious, good man, so he carefully maintained the worshipping of God in his house; that three times every day he called his family together in the solemnest manner to read to them, and pray to God with them, always committing them with the utmost affection and humility to the Divine protection, and casting themselves into the arms of God's infinite mercy. Twice every week they kept a solemn day, giving themselves up to God by fasting and prayer. Every night, indeed, looking on themselves as dead bodies, they lay down with dismal apprehensions, but were still comforted with finding themselves every morning preserved and in health. The careful father was up every morning the first in the house, and went to every chamber

[63]

PREPARATIONS FOR THE PLAGUE

door, servants as well as children, to ask them how they did; and when they answered, " Very well," left them with that short return, "Give God thanks." This he did, that if any had been ill they might immediately have been removed upstairs, as is mentioned above.

Hitherto he had corresponded with several of his acquaintances and customers in the country, and had received letters from them, and written letters to them constantly, but would not do any business, or send any goods to them upon any account, though very much pressed to it, because he resolved not to open his doors, whatever damages he suffered.

His letters were brought by the postman, or letter-carrier, to his porter, when he caused the porter to smoke them with brimstone and with gunpowder, then open them, and to sprinkle them with vinegar; then he had them drawn up by the pulley, then smoked again with strong perfumes, and, taking them with a pair of hair gloves, the hair outermost, he read them with a large reading-glass which read at a great distance, and, as soon as they were read, burned them in the fire; and at last, the distemper raging more and more, he forbid his friends writing to him at all.

In the height of this calamity, and when, as before, the good man was almost discouraged, he was still more straitened by the loss of his poor faithful porter. He missed him at the usual time when he was wont to lower down by the pulley a mess of broth to him, or some other thing warm for his breakfast; but calling to him he did not answer,

PREPARATIONS FOR THE PLAGUE

which made him afraid something was amiss with him. However, he heard nothing of him all that day or the next, when the third day, calling again from within the door for him, they were answered by a strange voice, who spoke in a melancholy tone that Abraham the porter was dead. "And who, then, are you?" said the master to the person that spoke. "I am his poor distressed widow, sir," says the answerer, "come to tell you that your poor servant is gone." He was greatly afflicted at the loss of so useful and so faithful a person. However, he composed himself. "Alas, poor woman," says he to her, "and what canst thou do, then?" "Oh, sir," says she, "I am provided for, I have the distemper upon me, I shall not be long after him."

He was perfectly astonished and surprised at her last words, and, as he said, it made his heart cold within him. However, as he stood surrounded by the smoke of gunpowder, and within the wooden shutter, he did not immediately retire, but said to her again, "If you are in such a condition, good woman, why did you come out?" "I came," she says, "sir, because I knew you would want poor Abraham to wait at your door, and I would let you know." "Well, but," says he, "if he is dead, I must want him; you cannot help me that are in such a condition as you speak of." "No, sir," says she, "I cannot help you, but I have brought you an honest poor man here that will serve you as honestly as poor Abraham did." "That is kindly done," said the master; "but how do I know what he is, and as he comes with you that are sick, as you say, how do

PREPARATIONS FOR THE PLAGUE

I know that he is not infected? I shall not dare to touch anything that comes from him." "Oh, sir," says she, "he is one of the safe men, for he has had the distemper and is recovered, so he is out of danger, or else I would not have brought him to you; he will be very honest."

This was an encouragement to him, and he was very glad of the new man; but would not believe the story of his being recovered till he brought the constable of the parish where he lived and another person to vouch for it. While this was doing, the poor woman, after some further questions and some money thrown down to her for relief, went away.

It was observable now that whereas they found, as is said above, that it was very melancholy at first to hear so many knells going continually, so on a sudden they now observed that there was not one knell to be heard; the reason, as his new porter told him, was that the number of those that died was so great, that they had forbid the bells ringing for anybody, and people were all fetched away by the carts, rich as well as poor. Many thousands of people would now have fled away if they could, but nobody would let them pass, and the enclosed family began to be in great terror; for the houses were desolated round about them, the numbers of people that died were scarce to be reckoned up, the bills gave an account of nearly fifteen hundred a week within the walls, notwithstanding the infinite number of people that were gone away into the country, so that it was his (the master's) opinion, that there would not one soul remain in the whole city, but that all would perish.

PREPARATIONS FOR THE PLAGUE

However, he concealed his fears as well as he was able, and continued as well his care over his family as his earnest prayers to God every day, and, as I may say, every hour for them.

In the midst of this misery, and as he began to be very well pleased and much assisted with his new porter, and particularly that he was one that having had the distemper, he concluded there was no danger of his having it again, — I say, in the midst of this he was surprised with a near affliction, for calling one morning to his new porter, nobody answered; he called several times again, and all that day and the next he heard nothing of him. But all the satisfaction he could get was from a watchman, who stood at the door of a house that was shut up, for all such houses had "Lord, have mercy," and a great cross set on the door, and a watchman placed without to prevent any one coming out or going in. The watchman, hearing the master of the house call the porter by his name, answered, and told him the poor man that used to stand at the door was sick of the plague, and he supposed was dead. The master answered, "I know he was sick that I had first, and is dead; but this was another." "Well, sir," says the watchman, "but he may be sick and dead too, I suppose, as well as the first." "No, no," says the master, "you must mistake, you mean the first." "No, sir," says the watchman; "I knew your first man Abraham was dead; but this man was called Thomas Molins, was he not?" "Yes," says the master. "Then, it is he I mean," says the watchman. "Why, that cannot be," says the master; "he had been ill of the plague before and was recovered, and he cannot have it again." "Alas! sir," says the watchman, "'t is that, I suppose, makes you so hard to understand me. I know 't is many people's opinion that when any has had it and recover they are secure; but, I assure you, it is a mistake, for I have been twice recovered of it in the pest-house, and been well a fortnight between the whiles, and now I am abroad again; but I don't think myself safe at all by that, for I know several that have had it three or four times, and some that have recovered three or four times have notwithstanding died of it afterwards." "And is my porter Molins sick of it again?" says the master. "Yes, sir," says the watchman, "I heard he was; but I will acquaint you more particularly tomorrow."

Accordingly the next day he called to the watchman again, who told him that he had inquired, and found that poor Molins, the porter, was carried away by the dead-carts, as they called them, the night before. He was surprised exceedingly at this, and shut the wooden door immediately without speaking a word more to him; and going in, sat him down, grieved most heartily, and wept by himself a great while to think that two poor men had thus lost their lives, as it were, to preserve him.

After some time he considered that there was no room for him to be discouraged, so went to his wife and took a large glass of Canary, which was his usual cordial, and putting as good a countenance on it as he could, said nothing of the death of the poor man

PREPARATIONS FOR THE PLAGUE

to his family, but resolved to remain quietly in the condition he was in; and as it pleased God that all his house continued in pretty good health, he considered that he had great reason to be comforted and thankful for that, and not to have any sorrows for others to affect his mind.

In this posture he remained about a fortnight more, having no manner of correspondence with the street, and he resolved to have no more porters; so he was perfectly without intelligence, except that still he found the watchman he had formerly talked with every day before the door of the house, as he thought, where he was at first.

[margin: V. good idea]

But after about a fortnight he grew impatient with being so entirely without intelligence and seeing none of the weekly bills, not knowing or hearing anything but the doleful noise of the dead-cart and the bell. At the end, I say, of the fortnight he opened his wooden window, and called to the watchman, asked him how he did, and how that house did where he was placed, supposing it the same where he was before. "Alas! master," says the poor man, "the distressed family are all dead and gone except the journeyman, and he is carried to the pest-house, and I am placed at Mr. ——'s at the next door, and they have three people sick and one dead."

[margin: desperation overcomes prudence.]

He asked him then, in general, how it went in the city. He told him, very bad; that the last week's bill was above eight thousand of all distempers; that it decreased at the other end of the town in St. Giles and in Holborn, the people being most of them dead or gone away; but that it increased dreadfully towards Aldgate and Stepney, and also in Southwark, where it had been more moderate before than in any other part of the town.

In a word, this being the middle of September, the plague was now in its utmost fury and rage, only that, as above, it was abated in the west end of the town, where it began; and, as the poor man told him, it had decreased a little in Cripplegate parish, though there still died in that parish between four and five hundred a week, and in the parish of Stepney above eight hundred a week.

It was heavy news to this poor gentleman to hear to what a dreadful height the calamity was come, and yet it was some encouragement that it had begun to go off to the eastward, and that it had decreased so much in Cripplegate parish, and he failed not to let his family know it; but still as the houses on both sides of him, and almost the whole row on the side over against him, were distempered, and some whole families dead, it was very terrible to them to think how they yet lived in the midst of death. His family began now to be sorely afflicted for want of air for breath, and, with continued eating of salt meats, began to grow scorbutic and out of order. He did what he could by desiring them to stir and be active and busy about the house to preserve health, but by no means suffered any window or door to be opened; but as the weather began to be cooler than it had been, he continued to keep fires in every room on that floor where they lodged, and had two of his family, who by turns sat up half a night, and two more the other half of the night,

PREPARATIONS FOR THE PLAGUE

every night to keep the fires in, and watch the house for fear of mischief.

This scorbutic illness increased pretty much upon them, but was greatly relieved at last by his accidental reading one day of people being cured of the scurvy at our islands Antigua or Nevis, by eating green lemons, after a long becalmed voyage from Guinea. Upon this he remembered that he had a quantity of lime juice and lemon juice in the house, which he gave plentifully about to the family, as often as they would drink it, and in about a week or ten days' time they found themselves sensibly bettered by the taking it.

The streets were now a melancholy sight to look into, the pavement was overgrown with grass; it was not one time in twenty that they looked through the glass (for they never opened any casement) that they could see anybody going along, or so much as a door open; as for the shops, they were all shut close, except that the apothecaries' and chandlers' shops kept a door open for the letting people come for what they wanted; not a coach or a cart to be seen, except now and then a coach carrying a sick body to the pest-house; and every night, three or four times a night, the dead-cart, with the bellman crying, "Bring out your dead."

The poor man was now so impatient for want of his porter that he could not content himself without opening his wooden window two or three times after this to talk with the watchman, who continued posted at the door of the house that was shut up, and to inform himself how things went; but at last he looked

PREPARATIONS FOR THE PLAGUE

for him and found he was gone too, which was a great loss to him, and he was the more troubled, because he intended to have given him some money.

But one day as he was looking through the glass, he spied the man standing on the other side of the street, and looking up towards his house; upon which he ran immediately to his wooden window, and opened it, though not forgetting to make the usual smoke with gunpowder for his preservation. When he had opened the door, the poor watchman told him he was glad to see him still alive, and that he had come twice before in hopes to see him, but was afraid he had not been well; that he came to tell him that he was dismissed from the house he was set to watch, most of the poor people being dead; and that if he pleased to accept it, he would sit at his door in the daytime, as his two porters had done.

He was glad of his offer, for he had not been easy for some time with being without; so he answered him, that he was glad to see him again, that he might give him something for what he had done for him in telling him how things were; so he threw the poor man two crowns, for which he was very thankful; after which he accepted his offer, and he took his post at the door as the others had done before; but he would not let him go to the post-house at all, or to any other place, only to give him intelligence of things as he heard them among his neighbours.

He had not been at the door many days but he called to his master and told him that he was glad to give him the good news that the infection abated, and that the weekly bill was now decreased 1837 in

PREPARATIONS FOR THE PLAGUE

one week, which had of a sudden given a great deal of joy among the people; that the burials in Cripplegate parish were sunk to within 200, though in Stepney parish they were still as high as ever, being between 800 and 900.

He failed not to run to his wife and family with this good news, but was fain to moderate it too, for that his sons began to be impatient to go abroad, which, however, he was resolved not to suffer. This was about the last week in September.

The next week his new porter gave him notice that the plague continued to abate, that the bill of mortality was again decreased between 600 and 700 more, though they were yet at a frightful height, being 5725 in a week, of all diseases.

However, it was a comfortable thing to think that the violence of the distemper began to assuage; and more especially that it abated in the part of the city, for in this last bill the burials in Cripplegate parish of all distempers came to but 196, which was but very few compared to 886 a week, which had died there a few weeks before. So that the plague was as much ceased to them as it would have been to the whole city, if there had not died above 1000 or 1200 per week.

His sons would fain have had him now, like Noah, have sent out a dove, that is, to have let them have gone out of doors to have seen how things were, and how the city looked; and they urged him the more, because they began to hear a noise of people in the streets passing to and fro, and that pretty often; but he kept his guard, and would not let any one

[73]

stir out on any terms, or on any pretence whatsoever.

The next week but two, which was the third in October, there was another decrease of 1849 in one bill; and now his porter knocked at his door (they did not open either door or wicket, but spoke to him), and he told them he desired to speak to his master, to tell him some good news. The master of the family soon appeared at his usual wooden window, with one of his sons, and one of his daughters. The watchman told him that now he hoped he could assure him that the visitation was really going off; that there had died 1849 less the last week than the week before, and that the Lord Mayor had ordered the carts to cease going about, except twice a week in several parts of the city, and in others but once each night; and that there had died but eighty-eight in Cripplegate parish that week of all diseases; that indeed it continued very high in Stepney, and especially in Southwark, but that in the city it was extremely abated.

He let down to the poor man, for his good news, a pint bottle of good sack, and a small basket with provisions for him and his family. And now they turned their two days of fasting, which they had constantly kept in the family every week, into one day of fasting and one day of thanksgiving, when on the sudden, to the great surprise of the whole family, the master himself, who was the life and spring of all the rest, and of all the management, which, under God, had so evidently preserved them, — I say, the master himself was taken very sick.

PREPARATIONS FOR THE PLAGUE

It is not for me at this distance to describe the terrible consternation they were all in. Not only the whole family, but the master himself, concluded he was struck with the plague. And through apprehension lest he should be the means to give it to any of his children, he would oblige them to have him carried out to the pest-house. His wife and all the children declared against it, and protested to him, every one of them, that they would rather have the distemper with him, and leave the consequence to God's mercy.

With these importunities he was prevailed with, but ordered a bed to be made immediately in one of the upper rooms mentioned before, and went presently to bed, taking such things as were prescribed publicly by the College of Physicians, to be given at any one's being first taken with the plague, which was to provoke sweat. Upon taking these things, he fell into a violent sweat immediately, and continued so all night. Any one may suppose the family had but little sleep that night, being in the utmost concern for so careful and so kind a father, as also very anxious to know whether their father had the distemper or no.

No more can I represent lively enough the joy there was in the house, when the next day they found their father had sweated very violently, fallen into a good sleep after it, and was so much refreshed and so well as to satisfy them all that his distemper was not at all infectious, but that it rather proceeded from the great weight and pressure of his cares, which had been too heavy for his spirits, and

[75]

PREPARATIONS FOR THE PLAGUE

withal, having taken some cold, as they thought, by standing too long talking at the wooden window to his watchman.

In short, the sweating had relieved him effectually, and in two or three days he was about house again and tolerably well, though weak by sweating a little too much.

While the master of the house lay thus, the family had no joy of the decrease of the plague; for what was the decrease to them if it broke out anew in their own house? But as soon as the master recovered a little, then they began to look abroad again for intelligence. And now they could see through their windows a new countenance of things in the streets and upon the houses; that the people began to go up and down the streets very frequently; and some began to open their shops, at least to open them half-way; the hackney coaches also were heard rumbling in the streets; so that without calling to the porter they could easily perceive that the distemper was greatly decreased, and that the people that were left had more courage than before, and, in a word, that the plague was going off, at least in the city, and chiefly on that side where they lived.

Their porter or watchman confirmed it to them the next day, when the weekly bill came about, which he brought to them. The master contented himself with hearing how it was, but would not let the bill be taken in, nor would he yet abate one tittle of his strict guarding his family from conversing with the streets by any means.

PREPARATIONS FOR THE PLAGUE

It was now the last week in October, and so greatly was the plague decreased, that there was but twenty-two buried of it in all Cripplegate parish, and but twenty-eight the week before, which was almost as surprising as the great rise of it at first; though even this week the bills were high in Stepney parish and in Southwark also.

Now, though this was joyful news to this as well as to other families, yet he was as anxious about the danger of opening his doors too soon, as he was before of keeping them open at first too long. He was aware that people would be rash in their joy, and that presuming on the health of the city being re-established, they would return to their houses and bring out their goods on which others had died, and air them too soon, and so perhaps bring back the infection. And it was just as he had said, for about the middle of November the bills on a sudden increased 400 at once, and rose from 1000 to 1400, and the city was in a terrible fright upon this occasion.

But it pleased God that it went off again, and the weather coming in cool, the distemper abated again, and the bills continued decreasing till in the third week of November they were once more under 1000 a week of all distempers, whereof but 652 of the plague.

It is true that, considering the number of people who were dead, which was very near 100,000, and the great number fled away, which, according to the most moderate guess, was at least three times as many; considering the numbers who had had the distemper and were recovered, who though, as was evident in the case of the second porter, they were not entirely free from the return of the distemper, yet they were not so very easily infected as others, — I say, considering this, the dying of 652 a week now was as much as the dying of 2000 a week was at the beginning of August; and this made him continue his caution with the same rigour as ever, and indeed with rather more; for he remembered well what a consternation the people were everywhere in when the plague was so increased as to die from 800 to 1000 a week of all distempers; and even this week I now speak of, which was from the 14th of November to the 21st, the bill stood at 905, whereof 652 of the plague.

Besides, there died in the city of the plague that very week above twice the number as died in the week from 21st to the 28th of July, when the bill was 1761 in all; for then there died but 56 in all the city within the walls, whereas now there died 127, I mean of the plague, so that the city was not so healthy then as the outparts. For example, the great parish of Cripplegate was so strangely restored, that there died in the week from the 21st to the 28th of November no more than ten persons in all, and but two of them of the plague; which perhaps was the least number that had been known in that parish before or since for above an hundred years.

All these things he calculated exactly, and, as he said, was very loth to lose all the fruit of his care and caution, and of the close confinement he had submitted to, — I say, he was very loth to lose it all at once by a rash and needless adventure. His reasons were so

PREPARATIONS FOR THE PLAGUE

good, and their own safety so much concerned in it, that his family submitted to it with the more cheerfulness, though they began to labour hard for breath at that time, and to be very desirous of air, having been shut up so close and so long, as above.

The first of December, like Noah, who opened the window of the Ark to send out his dove, he opened his street door for the first time and walked out. The bill of mortality the week before was 544 of all diseases, whereof only 333 of the plague, whereof nearly half of that number were out of Stepney parish, and the Southwark side of the river, where the sickness continued longest, and was longest before it began.

The first of December, I say, he walked out, but suffered none of his family to stir but himself; he viewed the streets, the houses and shops, but conversed with nobody, nor did he see anybody that he knew, except a few just in his own neighbourhood. A vast number of houses were standing empty and deserted, the inhabitants being gone into the country; yet in some of those he observed servants, returned, who had opened the windows and doors, and were, as we call it, airing the houses and the goods, making fires in all the rooms, opening the windows, and burning perfumes in the rooms, preparing them in that manner for the return of the families that belonged to them.

The numbers of people in the streets were greater indeed than he expected; but this seemed to be occasioned rather by the curiosity of the people which were left, which led them to go more abroad than

PREPARATIONS FOR THE PLAGUE

otherwise they would have done, for in the back streets and ways less frequented he found very few people.

He came home again in a few hours, not having visited anybody, or made any inquiries after any of his friends, or any one else, and resolved to keep up to his close quarters one week longer; nor would he buy any fresh provisions, or suffer any one to go to market, but resolved upon some new measures which he put in practice the week following. He went out early in the morning, and taking his eldest son and his apprentice with him, they walked on foot as far as Tottenham High Cross, and finding a house there of one of his acquaintance, which had not been affected at all, he took lodgings or apartments in it for his whole family, and the same day returned to London. The same week he removed them all thither, carrying his own goods and some part of his own provisions; all which he caused to be fetched by waggons belonging to the country people, and such as he had good information were sound and had not been infected at all.

Here he not only relieved his family with fresh air, which they so much wanted, but with fresh provisions also, which he had now brought to them from Waltham Market by his old higgler who had supplied the family at the beginning of the year.

He left his house at London fast locked up, except the gate in his yard, the key of which he gave to the honest watchman, and went himself, or his son, or his apprentice, two or three times a week, to see that everything was safe and in good order. And thus

WHEN THE PLAGUE BEGAN TO ABATE

The first of December, I say, he walked out, but suffered none of his family to stir but himself

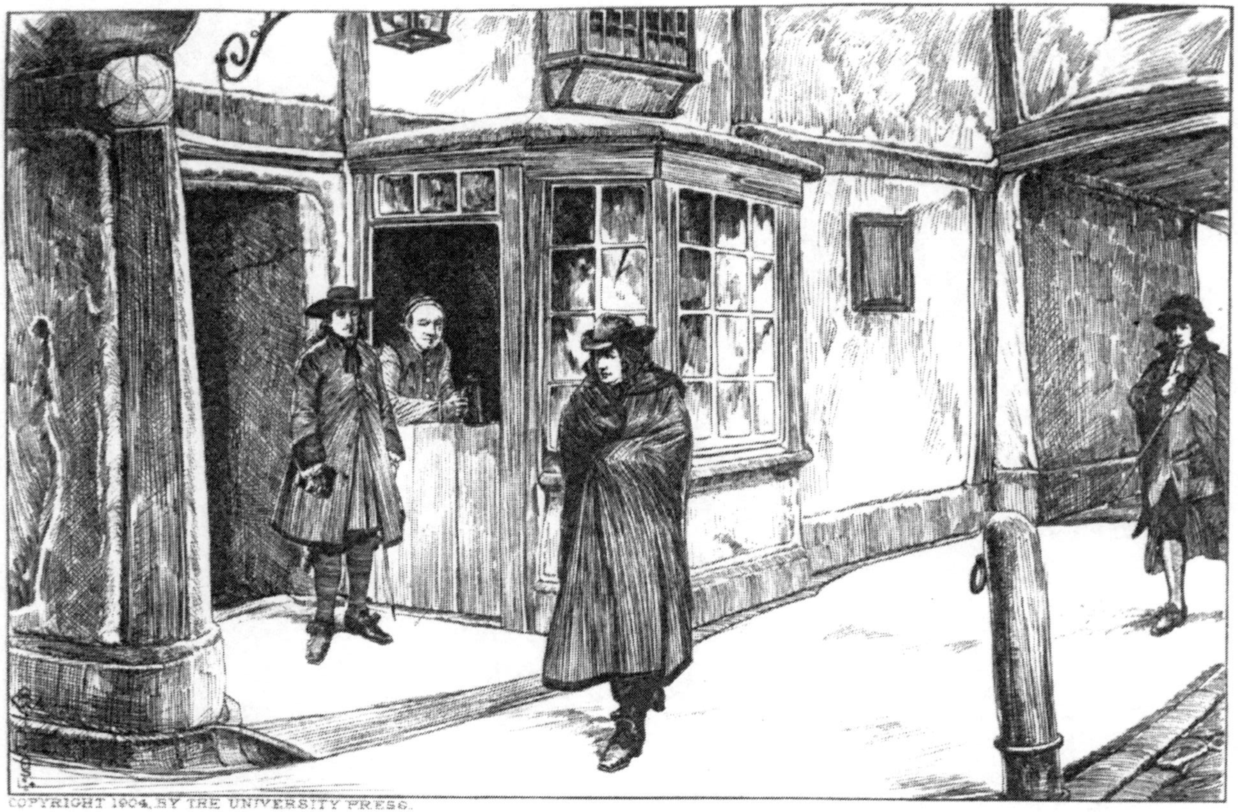

PREPARATIONS FOR THE PLAGUE

he continued till the February following; for all the months of December and January the plague continued in the city, and at the latter end of December it began to increase again, which was believed to be by the people's returning faster than ordinary to their dwellings; so that the third week in December the number increased was 83, and there died of the plague still 281, the whole bill being 525.

But by the beginning of February, the family being well recovered and refreshed, and all in perfect health, and the city being filled again with people, and in pretty good state of health, he removed all back again, and came to his house, opened his doors, and carried on his business as before.

Thus, next under the protection of God's providence, a complete retirement from the street, and from conversing on any account whatever with the rest of the people, separating from them, and having, as we may say, nothing to do with them, neither to buy or sell, or speak or sit with or near them, has been approved to be capable of effectually preserving a man or a family in the time of an infection.

I will not suppose this man or his family, who were so severe in fasting and humbling themselves before God all the time they were under apprehensions of the distemper, and surrounded with daily experience of the dreadful calamity that lay upon the city, could so far forget themselves now as not to give God thanks in the most solemn manner possible for their deliverance. That part I take for granted; they could not be rational creatures any more than Christians and retain no sense of so signal preservation. I

PREPARATIONS FOR THE PLAGUE

will therefore, I say, take that for granted, and suggest that the master of the family, with the utmost seriousness and devotion, performed this part, and that he obliged all his family to do the like.

Here is now a perfect rule for any one to walk by, and to preserve themselves against the most violent infection that ever yet happened in this nation, for such I esteem that plague to be. And I judge it by this, that although we call it a plague year, and that the number of persons that died is accounted to the whole year, that is, from the 20th of December 1664 to the 20th of December 1665, yet the gross part of the number perished within the compass of less than four months, namely, from the 18th of July to the 14th of November, in which time there died 81,559 people of all distempers; whereas the whole number in the twelve months, as by the yearly bills, amounts to but 97,306. Or take it of the numbers reckoned to die of the plague, and brought in so by the bill of mortality, the whole number that died of the plague in the year from the 20th of December 1664 to the 19th of December 1665 was 68,596, whereof there died in the compass of the four months above mentioned, from the 18th of July to the 14th of November, 65,045. So that in the whole seven months of January, February, March, April, May, June, and December, and half July and half November, there died of the plague 3551, and no more.

Again, in nine weeks of these four months the violence of this contagion was indeed most dreadful, and beyond all that ever was before in this nation. For example, from the 9th of August to the 16th of

PREPARATIONS FOR THE PLAGUE

October there was buried 60,410 persons, an incredible number, if we consider that, by the judgment of all that have been seriously inquisitive in that matter, the bills of mortality neither did, nor was it possible, as circumstances were then known to be, that they should give a full account of the numbers of people that perished in that dreadful calamity. Many perished in the fields and highways, wandering in their distress and desperation from the town, desolate and not knowing whither to go; the villages adjacent also refusing to suffer them to come in, or to give them any shelter. Thousands perished in those towns adjacent to London which are not included in the bills of mortality, which were, notwithstanding, crowded with people who fled thither from London in the beginning of the infection, expecting safety there; which, however, the distemper being so violent, was little protection to them, and they rather assisted to make those towns more unhealthy than they would perhaps have otherwise been. These towns are said to have buried above 5000 people, some think many more, such as follows:—

Chelsea.	Tottenham.	Deptford.
Kensington.	Newington.	Lewisham.
Knightsbridge.	Walthamstow.	Peckham.
Hammersmith.	Low Leyton.	Camberwell.
Fulham.	Stratford.	Clapham.
Brentford.	East & West Ham.	Battersea.
Chiswick.	Barking.	Putney.
Pancras.	Ilford.	Wimbledon.
Paddington.	Wanstead.	Wandsworth.
Hampstead.	Woolwich.	Tooting.
Hornsey.	Greenwich.	Mitcham.
Edmonton.	Eltham.	Streatham.

PREPARATIONS FOR THE PLAGUE

Yet, in this dreadful visitation, a retreat has been effectual in the very city, and doubtless would still be so if managed with the same prudence at another time.

Here is the example. The pattern contains complete directions; and I cannot doubt but if the same method were taken by any family, the same security would, by the blessing of God, be obtained.

I am to observe, that whereas this gentleman laid in a magazine of stores sufficient for his family, I mean provisions for a whole year, so, as he was not shut up above seven months, he had a great quantity of biscuit, beer, cheese, beef, and other things remaining.

If his stores were short in anything 'twas in fine flour and butter, but the reason was not that he had not duly proportioned everything for an equal supply, but that his wife, his children, and indeed servants and all, having not been used to the coarse hard biscuit-bread, could at first scarce bite it with their teeth, and contrived abundance of small things, puddings and pies, and cakes of several sorts, and bread such as their own little oven would bake; only that, wanting yeast, they could not supply themselves with such bread as they usually had, but were obliged to make it heavy and sad, not knowing how to leaven their bread, as some countries do. On the other hand, they mingled butter and sometimes fine oil with their flour, and made an abundance of baked things to supply the place with bread, and this was the reason of their flour not holding out so well as their bread.

PREPARATIONS FOR THE PLAGUE

However, as I may suppose, when he brought his family home again, and the markets were open and provisions came in plenty again, and might be eaten freely, he brought out what was left of his magazine, that is to say, of the eatables and liquids, and made a thank-offering of it to the poor; nor was it a small quantity in the whole, seeing he had left —

    1500 lb. weight of bread.
    5 hogsheads of his beer.
    300 lb. weight of cheese.
    5 flitches of bacon.
    2 barrels and a piece of salted beef.
    No pork and no butter or flour.

This account is given the more largely, because it may stand as a mark of direction, which will not merit any exception in the manner. And I can assure my reader that several families have been preserved in this late dreadful plague at Marseilles by the same method; and I have seen letters from thence full of the particulars, and acknowledging the success.

It is true that the poorer inhabitants are not able to do thus, and, therefore, this example, or this advice, does not immediately reach to them. But, as in the first part of this work, I have mentioned what care might, and indeed ought to be taken of the poor, viz., to remove their wives and children, to keep and succour them in particular, separating them from the rest, — I say, that then would the remaining inhabitants, who were able thus to retreat, do it in the manner as here described, they would necessarily employ so many of the men who should remain

PREPARATIONS FOR THE PLAGUE

as porters and watchmen at their doors, and subsist them with provisions from within, that even those poor men would not be exposed to the conversing with one another, which is the fatal part in such extremities as these.

It is nothing but the necessity of going about among one another which prompts the contagion, and extends it into every corner of the city. If the poor could live within doors, as the rich may, the poor would be as safe as the rich are, but that necessity that sends them abroad to get their bread brings them home infected.

It is not so much the poor living close and not cleanly that infects them. Their dirty clothes and uncomfortable lodgings and hard fare does not give them the plague, does not infect them. If so, they would never be without it. I will not say but that it makes their cure more difficult, and want of food and of physic makes them sink under it, when they have it; but it is their going abroad among one another that infects them, and then want of conveniences and of being assisted and looked after causes them to perish faster than others.

The whole scheme of my discourse, therefore, aims at separating the people as much as possible from one another, and on this depends their safety and health; I mean as to second causes, and the means of preserving it. As to the agency of Providence, I am no way invading it, or impeaching the wisdom of Heaven in the directing these things.

I must say I reject, though with decency, the notions of those people who take upon them to tell

PREPARATIONS FOR THE PLAGUE

us that the plague is not conveyed by contagion from the bodies infected. It seems to me to be an ill-grounded hypothesis, argued upon as the persons who espouse those notions think fit; and as the opinion is boldly advanced against the universal experience of mankind for many ages, I leave them to be confuted by the same experience.

However, to avoid cavilling, or making this work, which is written with a better design, a scene of debate, I leave them to their own notions, and those that please to believe them may venture their lives upon the faith of it, if they think fit; but I believe few will. And, in the meantime, I acknowledge, as at the beginning, that I write this upon a supposition of the common hypothesis, namely, that the distemper is what we call catching or contagious; that is to say, the sound are infected by the sick, let it be in what manner they please, whether by effluvia from their bodies, by animalcula mixed and drawn into our bodies with our breath, or by the venom of the tumours, blains, and sores, or how you please; and that conversing with those who are infected gives the infection, which is propagated in that manner from one to another. I say, I laid down this as a principle which experience and the judgment of very able physicians and men of long practice confirm to me, whose authority I must needs say I have not yet seen overthrown; and as the history I have given of a family preserved by retiring from conversation is really the history of several families rather than of one, and is a perfect model for future practice, I think that account, with several others which I could give, within the compass of my own knowledge, or the particulars thereof I have had from the persons of credit, — I say, these are convincing proofs to me at least of what I build upon, namely, that the distemper is taken by contagion from the diseased bodies. Let those who believe otherwise act as they see fit; but let them remember that they cannot say they have wanted precaution, derived from innumerable examples of those who have been infected by their conversing with others.

I must confess, I think the publishing such a vast variety of opinions in this case as we see every day brought to light, is like publishing the cavils and opinions of divines in the great dispute about the Trinity, dangerous instead of directing to the readers; amusing the people so that (though in the most important article of religion) they know not what to conclude, or which opinion to accept.

In like manner here, in the most important article of our health we are so perplexed with the opinions of the physicians; some declaring the plague not dangerous in one way, and some that it is most dangerous in other ways; while by common experience we find it dangerous every way; and this carried up to such a degree as it is, that we know not whom to follow, or whom to give credit to.

My short judgment, and which I leave to experience, is this, that be the bodies of sick persons infectious or not, be it safe to visit and converse with them or be it not, things which we may never determine in theory, this is certain, that in declining conversation with the sick, nay, in declining all communication with one another in time of infection, there can be but little error, and 't is the much safer way for all people to act; in the negative there can be no danger; the retreat then, which I recommend, must be acknowledged to be the most innocent mistake that man or family can commit.

It is a fine notion, if I had said a fine-spun notion I had been excusable, to say that we are in no danger of infection from conversing with infected bodies; but who do these gentlemen think they shall persuade to run the hazard of the experiment? Nay, will the gentlemen themselves show us the way? and if they should, we must see through the whole visitation before we can tell whether they are in the right or not.

Nay, if it should happen that any bold adventurer should thus hazard the experiment and live, even then it does not prove the thing to be true, for he may live and not be infected, and yet I may catch it at the first attempt and be lost. Perhaps this man's constitution, or precautions, or particular conduct, or his fate may prevent him being infected, but yours or mine may not. There are infinite numbers perish in a plague, that is true, and this convinces us that it is a contagion conveyed from and catched of one another; yet in the hottest and highest infection that ever was, some have escaped and never been infected at all, although they may have lived among the infected bodies all the time. I knew a sexton and bearer of a parish in London who dug all the graves, and helped to carry all the bodies that were carried in coffins to the grave, in the whole parish he lived in, and yet never had the distemper, and the like instances of many others; but this is as far from proving that the distemper is not infecting, as it proves that musket bullets do not kill men in an army, because all that are shot at or wounded do not die.

Some ascribe it to the goodness of Providence, and to a merciful disposition for the comfort of the citizens of London at that time, that the persons necessary to tend the sick, to bury the dead, and to assist in public matters, were preserved, and very seldom had the plague, as nurses in the very chambers of the sick, and in the pest-houses, hospitals, &c., cart-drivers and bellmen that carried away the dead bodies in the night, and grave-diggers who assisted to bury them, and the like, and, as it was said, market people who brought provisions to market, and who, they say, never had the distemper.

But (1.), with due deference to oral tradition, this is a mistake. It is true, poor people pressed by their own circumstances, trade and workmanship being at a kind of full stop, were glad for bread at any hazard to undertake those dangerous and dismal offices of tending the sick and burying the dead; and in many cases the magistrates of the city obliged them to do it; but then it must be acknowledged that many did catch the distemper, and many of them died, though, as in other cases, not all of them.

(2.) After the sickness had been some time among us, as in all infections some died, so in this some had been infected and recovered; and though it is true that it did not perfectly secure them from a relapse,

PREPARATIONS FOR THE PLAGUE

or from having it a second or third time, or oftener, as it was found by experience, yet it was a general notion with the people that they could not have it twice, and that made such as had recovered be the bolder in offering themselves to those works; and perhaps, too, they were not so easily infected as others were, though they were not wholly secured. So that by the time the plague was come to its height most of the nurses and necessary people above were made up of such as had been infected and were recovered; and this particular circumstance recommended them to the families they were employed in, because they then thought they were safe from losing the nurse they had depended on, having her die in the house, or having her carried away when she was most wanted, and perhaps not any other to be had.

So that, upon the whole, those people not dying as others did is very far from being a convincing reason that the plague was not contagious, &c.; as to the market people, higglers who brought provisions to London, being so singularly preserved by Heaven in mercy to the distressed citizens, that none of them had the plague or carried it home to their families, I would be very far from lessening so great and valuable a memorial of merciful heaven, and of His care for the good of His afflicted creatures, if I were sure of the fact; but as I have never met with sufficient authority for the thing, or had it proved so as I might depend upon the truth of it, I shall say no more than this to it: that as those who relate it look upon it to be little less than miraculous, so as such I should receive it if it was proved to be true;

PREPARATIONS FOR THE PLAGUE

but if it were true, it neither way proves that the distemper was not catching.

But to come a little nearer home, if this were true, what mean the physicians and the Government in France at this time? And what are they doing there in surrounding the towns which are visited with their soldiers, keeping in the sound with the sick till they all perish together? What need of the dreadful severities they have used there, in shooting dead so many innocent people, who, made desperate by their danger, have attempted to escape either by force or secretly, and get away, if possible, out of the danger? If the poor, desperate creatures did not see that to be locked up there among the infected people was present death to them, and that they would be unavoidably infected and lost, what pushes them upon such desperate attempts for escape, in which they are almost sure to be discovered, and, if discovered, are sure to be killed without mercy? I say, what can push them upon such desperate things but the apparent knowledge of the distemper being catching from the bodies of their friends who are infected?

On the other hand, why such severities, nay, cruelties and barbarities (for if there was no reason for them they must be called such), as shooting to death two poor, innocent children who, in mere duty to their distressed father, who lay sick in the mountains, found means to pass the lines in Dauphine in the night, and go to him to carry him relief, which two poor children, one thirteen years old and one fourteen, were shot without mercy, and against the entreaties and cries of the very inhabitants where they were taken? What need, I say, of such inexorable cruelty if necessity and the just fear of infection from the bodies of those miserable creatures did not make it justifiable?

I might instance many other acts of severity, such as shooting five soldiers who had the guard of the lines, for having pursued two sheep to kill them within the lines, lest they should get back and infect the country, so that the poor men were killed for their extraordinary diligence in their duty. There are more stories of the like nature which we have had publicly printed and written, but as I cannot depend on the truth of the particulars, I omit them. The general part, namely, that they do practise things, and do shoot and put to death all that attempt to escape if they come within their reach, is undoubted.

Now 't is certain the French, who are a nation of humanity, would never exercise such severities upon their own people — I mean they would not as a nation, and as a Government under wholesome laws — if they were not fully satisfied that the contagion of this distemper is thus conveyed from the bodies of the infected to the bodies of the sound, and that it was dangerous for the sound to converse with the sick.

This opinion of theirs 't is evident all their physicians come into, and it is allowed that the French Court is not ill-furnished with gentlemen that have made the greatest proficiency in the knowledge of medicine, and in the study of distempers, of any nation whatsoever.

Nor is it the opinion of the physicians there only, but the same notion is entertained by all the Christian world, as appears by the prohibiting commerce and even conversation with any person coming from France; which, it is plain, proceeds from the apprehensions lest those people should be already infected with the distemper, and should communicate it from their particular bodies to the people they come among.

Now, if it was true, as these men insinuate, that no contagion can be conveyed from one body to another, then all the nations in Christendom proceed at present upon wrong notions. All the people they kill in the severities I speak of are unjustly and injuriously killed, and there are just so many cold-blood murders committed by them; likewise all the measures taken to keep the people in the places infected from coming among the people that are sound and not infected, are ridiculous and to no purpose.

I shall say no more to this matter; the contrary is an amusement, and, if I may give my opinion, cannot extend very far, nor will the gentlemen that have advanced it, I believe, get many friends to it, at least not such as will venture their lives upon the credit of the opinion.

On the other hand, if I go on a mistake, I err in much good company, for I have the practice of the whole Christian world on my side. Nay, though I were to grant it was a mistake, which, however, I can by no means do, yet I am right in my proposals, in that I am laying down rules for the preservation of mankind upon the foot of that same principle which they all go upon, namely, that of the distemper being infectious, that is to say, that the infection is taken from one to another by the infected bodies emitting

PREPARATIONS FOR THE PLAGUE

poisonous particles either from the pores of the body or from the breath, or from some malignant effluvia which pass from the body infected and are received by the body at that time to be infected; when the world may, by the introducing this new opinion, change their methods universally, then, and not before, the scheme I lay down may be voted useless. I might proceed to some common remedies or preservatives which have been found useful in times of infection to those whose circumstances would not permit them to retire from company and from conversing with their neighbours. But our physicians have crowded the world with medicines, as well simple as compound, and there is no room to say anything after them. However, as I have no notion, I must confess, of venturing among infected people without any preservative, I cannot but mention some of them. I have known that some have preserved themselves in the last plague, 1665, by only having a bottle of vinegar in their hands, and being continually smelling to it. I myself have rid through a town infected with the plague with a bunch of rue in my mouth, and have been secured; others have taken rue and wormwood together. I know a physician who visited several patients, even in the pest-house near London in 1665, and went freely into their chambers, but all the while he was in the rooms would be chewing a stalk of angelica in his mouth, and every morning, before he went among them, drank the quantity of an ordinary glass of Canary with the stalk of angelica steeped in it, and he never was infected so as to be quite sick with it.

PREPARATIONS FOR THE PLAGUE

Innumerable such prescriptions were to be had, built on the experience of many who have practised them, but nothing of all this ever comes up to the grand experiment which I have recommended in this work — I mean that of separating ourselves, and retiring wholly from conversation, whether in families or otherwise, and laying in store of provisions, to shut themselves as entirely up as if " Lord, have mercy," and a cross, was set on their door.

Frequent sweatings by those that are retired, as above, cannot but be very useful to them, as well for preventing the mischiefs which frequently follow being too closely confined and want of air, as to keep the body from any mischief received, or like to be received, from the nearness of the contagion; but then those sweatings should be very moderate and gentle, and chiefly occasioned by some little stirring and exercise, such as running up and down stairs, or any brisk motion, but with a first reserve against over-tiring the spirits or heating the blood.

I object nothing against the medicines prescribed by the physicians. Every one will act in that case as their opinion of the several physicians they use prompts them; all that I have thought needful of that kind I have tied down to preparative physic, as above. What is to be done when the distemper is come, when the body is infected and the distemper has seized the blood, that is not the business or design of this undertaking, nor does it come within the compass of what we call preparations.

When the blood is once tainted, and the body infected, preparations are then at an end. Then you must look upon the fortress as effectually besieged and formally attacked, and you must muster up all the strength of nature and art for your relief.

But this is not my part, as I have said; but having brought up the several states of health to this length, I leave it to talk of the other part — I mean preparations for the plague. What preparations I have mentioned yet are such as are needful to preserve the body from the plague. And when the person has the plague really upon him, I have no more to say but this: he must turn his thoughts another way, viz., he must make preparations for death; I see nothing else before him, nor ought he to expect anything else. And this brings me to the second part of my work.

PREPARATIONS FOR THE PLAGUE

This is the hardest part of the work by far; but of the two, infinitely of greater consequence, as the eternal state into which we are all to pass from this, is of more consequence than the present state.

Life and time are indeed of an inestimable value, but they are only so, or principally so, as on the happy conclusion of them depends the eternal welfare of the person to whom they are so valuable; and especially, the preparations for an eternal state are only to be made in time, which, once slipped away, lost and unapplied, is irrecoverably lost for ever.

The approaches of death are oftentimes imperceptible, and the attacks sudden; the distempers by

PREPARATIONS FOR THE PLAGUE

which we are carried away are violent; and it is a double terror to the dying person to have the work of dying and the work of repentance both upon his hands together. Oh, sinner! remember that the terrors of thy conscience will be a weight too heavy to be borne at the same time with the terrors of death. Nay, the terrors of conscience are those alone which give terrors of death, which make the passage out of life dreadful; and these many times make a disease mortal which would not otherwise be so. Were the diseases and casualties of which people frequently die in this populous city rightly given into the bills of mortality, many would be set down of other distempers than as we find them. Instead of hanged themselves (being distracted), and cut their own throats (being distracted), it would be said, hanged themselves (being in despair), and cut their own throats (being in dreadful trouble of mind); instead of pain in the head, it would be pain in the mind; instead of convulsions, it would be said, horror of conscience, and the like. I doubt not but these horrors I speak of throw the body into fevers and convulsions, and at least assist those distempers to destroy us. It is enough to have a violent fever drink up the moisture and life, and not to have the arrows of the Almighty drinking up the spirits; that, therefore, Christians may prepare in time for the dreadful moments which are approaching; that when the call is heard, no other noise may drown their comforts; and that the business of life may now without any delay be to prepare for death, — I say, that they may be moved to do thus, this tract is written.

PREPARATIONS FOR THE PLAGUE

The apprehensions we are under at this time of the approaching calamity which afflicts our neighbours, are a kind of summons to this preparation, and that more forcible than can be given from the mouth of man; and many thousands will have reason to be thankful for so long a warning, so timely a summons; even all those who listen to the voice of it. Let me add a mite to this treasury. The goodness of God is very conspicuous in this, that as a pestilence sweeps whole towns and cities of people away, and death rages like an overwhelming stream, that there is little or no time given for repentance or calling upon God — little time to look up or to look in — so that notice given of its approach ought to be taken for the time of interval, for both looking up and looking in, and be improved to that purpose.

Nay, so merciful is God to us, that we really have more time usually given to us in the case of a plague, I say, more time than we have in most sorts of other distempers, and that time blest with greater advantages. This is so much against the common notions we have of it, that it requires some explanation, but you will be more fully informed of it in a short discourse which happened between some relations in a family in London, just before the last great plague.

The time before that dreadful visitation was, as this is, a time of apprehension and terror; something like this, it is true, the warnings were not so long or the danger so very remote. The distemper, according to that eminent physician Dr. Hodges, was brought to Holland on board a ship, in some bales of goods from the Levant, I think from Smyrna, as this contagion now raging in France was said to be brought in bales of goods from Zidon and the Isle of Cyprus.

From Holland it came over hither; how it was brought over to us, or by who, that was never particularly known, or at least not publicly. The first that died of it here, at least that was put into the bills openly as dead of the plague, was in the parish of St. Giles-in-the-Fields. It was reported that the whole family died; and I have some reason to believe they did too, but there was but one entered in the weekly bill, and this was about December 1664.

This was Heaven's first alarm to the city of London, for it was remarkable that the infection began in the heart of the kingdom, as I may call it. It did not begin in a remote place, as has been the case in France, where it began at Marseilles, above 400 miles off Paris, and so came on gradually; but it first appeared in London itself, and, as I have said above, the first that was publicly given in in St. Giles's parish, about the 20th of December 1664. As this blow was near the heart, so it more nearly touched the people, and their apprehensions seemed to be in proportion more serious and affecting.

Two brothers and a sister, the children of one pious and serious mother, a widow, lived together in one house in the city; they were all grown to years of discretion, the sister (the youngest) being about nineteen, and one of the brothers near forty, the other about twenty-six years of age. The sister was a most religious and well-instructed young woman,

PREPARATIONS FOR THE PLAGUE

knowing in all religious and heavenly knowledge; the brothers men of business, engaged in it and taken much up with it. They had been religiously educated, and were what we call sober and orderly people, but being embarrassed in business and hurried in the world, getting money and growing rich, they had not made the concern of eternal life the chief business of the present life, as we all ought to do.

'Not saved'

The two gentlemen were merchants, had lived abroad, and being returned to England, were entered into great engagements of business, and had vast concerns on their hands; were partners, and had two or three servants and book-keepers that were daily in the counting-house and doing business, as well at the waterside as at the Royal Exchange with their masters.

As the eldest of the two brothers was a widower, and had but two children, who were very small, and that the youngest brother was a bachelor, the young lady their sister was their housekeeper, and they called her familiarly their governess; and such indeed she was many ways, being not only the guide of their whole family, which was large, but a faithful monitor to themselves also as occasions presented, though not at first with all the success that she wished for; their heads and hearts, as above, being wholly taken up with business and the world.

The old lady did not live in the house with them, but having two or three younger children with her, lived a little way out of town, having also two other sons, young gentlemen of about nineteen or twenty years of age, who were abroad in Spain or Italy, and

PREPARATIONS FOR THE PLAGUE

placed in very good business by the directions and on account of their brothers.

The good mother of this family, having early impressions of the danger that was impending, began to have a heavy heart, and be deeply concerned on account of her sons; and having received early impressions, as all the town indeed had, that a heavy and grievous judgment was coming upon the city, and upon the whole nation; and as she came frequently to town to her sons, which was, as it were, her other family, she failed not on every occasion to be putting them in mind what a stroke, as she said, was coming upon the nation, and upon the city in particular; and to let them know what a dismal time it would be with all those people especially whose eternal state was not secured, and who had not the comfort of a safe passage out of life in their view.

This she urged upon her children every time she came to see them, and particularly would be representing to them how it was in London in the time of the great plague, as it was then called, which had been twenty-nine years before, "which I," says she, "very well remember, having lived here all that while, and lost several relations and acquaintances who died of the infection, at which time there died 10,400 people of the plague in the city only; and likewise in the plague eleven years before that, viz., in 1624, when there died of all distempers above 54,000 people in London and the out parishes, not reckoning in the city of Westminster, or the parishes of Stepney, Hackney, Islington, Lambeth, Rotherhithe, or Christ Church, and Newington in Surrey."

PREPARATIONS FOR THE PLAGUE

She talked so often of it that her elder son used to tell her she was a little too positive; that it looked as if she would be thought prophetic; that the plague was not actually broken out because one man had died of it; that he believed it was always in one part or another of the city a little; that the plague in 1636, which she remembered, held eight years, and that every year there died, more or less, from 300 to 3000; that there was yet no publication of it, " and I hope, madam," says he, "there will not;" and therefore that we should not be always alarming one another as if it was at the door; that the calamity was terrible enough when it came, but that to be always in a fright about it, was to make it a judgment when it was no judgment, and the like; in a word, like her sister preachers, Mary Magdalene, &c., her "words seemed to them as idle tales" (Luke xxiv. 11).

However, like a true, affectionate mother, she continued her monitory discourses to them. "You, sons," says she, "are grown up, and are above my admonition as the mother, but you cannot be out of the reach of exhortation; and my speaking to you," says she, "is with so much regard to your years, that you ought not, however, to take it amiss that I press you to prepare for the dreadful time of a visitation if it should come."

"No, madam," says the eldest son, "none of your children will take it amiss; but we think you make your company, which was always pleasant to us, be a little melancholy, for that you are always upon this frightful subject. I doubt it is too much upon

PREPARATIONS FOR THE PLAGUE

your mind, and makes you heavy-hearted when you might be cheerful." And then their discourse began.

Mother. I cannot look back, child, without horror of mind upon the dreadful time in the year 1625. I was but newly married and settled in the world, and we were full of mirth as you are now, and on a sudden the distemper broke out, and all our smiles were turned into lamentations and tears.

Son. It came suddenly, it may be, without any warning?

Mother. No, no, people had warning too; but we that were young people then, just as you are now, we would take no notice of it. We were marrying and giving in marriage to the very day that it came upon us; and when good people spoke to us of repenting and preparing to meet the Lord in His day of wrath, and humble ourselves under His mighty hand, we thought them, just as you do now, too melancholy and phlegmatic; that they did not do well to alarm the people, and put families and cities into frights and disorders. And thus we went on.

Son. Well, madam, and yet for all that it may be you thought as seriously of it when it came as they did?

Mother. Ay, son; but they that had thought seriously of it so long before us had a great advantage of us, and were so much before us in their preparations.

Son. They had so much more, indeed, to answer for if they were not better prepared.

PREPARATIONS FOR THE PLAGUE

Mother. I think, son, it should be rather said we had so much the more to answer for if we were worse prepared.

Son. But, madam, what can we do in the case as it stands now? Every one ought to prepare for death whether there be a plague in the town or no. Death comes in many other shapes than that of a pestilence.

Mother. That is true, child; and I do not speak against daily preparations for death. God forbid I should. But when an infection comes, child, Death seems to come with more terrors about him, cuts down swifter, and we have less time to think what is to follow.

Son. Some reflect upon the severity of the judgment upon that very score, in that people are swept away with a stroke, and have scarce time to look up.

Mother. No, son, let none say so, for I affirm that God's mercies are so interspersed with His judgments that we have abundant cause to acknowledge them, and ought to keep our eye upon it in this particular, namely, that God always gives more time to people to prepare for death in the case of a plague than of an ordinary distemper.

Son. How, madam? That cannot be, for in the plague people often die in twelve hours after they are taken, whereas in fevers and other distempers they generally lie as many days or more.

Mother. Ay, son, but then you do not consider that the plague generally approaches a country by slow degrees, and you have many months' warning of it before it comes; so that if it swept all away in a

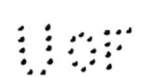

PREPARATIONS FOR THE PLAGUE

day, there is no room to call it severity, for every one had warning of it beforehand.

Son. But people do not look on the judgment at particular till it touches them personally, or that is points to them in a family capacity — that is to say, till it has gotten into the house.

Mother. That folks do not take warning is their folly and fault; but that God gives them warning is their mercy, if they know how to make use of it.

Son. Everybody is willing to hope they shall escape.

Mother. But everybody ought to provide as if they were not to escape. Every soldier in the army hopes to escape being killed, but every soldier puts on his headpiece that he may fare the better if he is hit.

Son. We should prepare, no doubt; but to be apprehensive continually, as if we were sure to have the distemper, is even to fright us into it. All physicians agree that we should keep our minds easy and calm; that the passions of fear and anger prepare the heart to receive and nourish the infection, at least to dispirit and debilitate it, so that it is not duly fortified and encouraged to resist the approaching enemy which it is to struggle with.

Mother. You greatly mistake the thing, child, and mistake my meaning. I am of the same mind, and say as the doctors do, though upon other grounds: the mind should be kept calm and free, that Nature might be assisted to repulse the enemy that attacks her. But then I say that nothing can animate and encourage the mind like a firm resignation to the will of God, and a comfortable hope that it shall be

PREPARATIONS FOR THE PLAGUE

well with us beyond life. This is certainly the best preparation for the distemper.

Son. I do not deny but we should be always preparing for death, but we should not be discouraging ourselves before it comes.

Mother. What do you call discouraging yourselves? Preparation is the only way to avoid being discouraged.

Son. You talk of preparation as if I was sure it would come upon me.

Mother. As soon as we have reason to be satisfied that the distemper is begun, and is among us, I think every one, speaking of his preparation, should look upon himself as if absolutely struck, as much as if he saw the tokens upon his flesh.

Son. And is not that all phlegmatic and vapours, madam? Do not many, do ye think, in the plague, as they do in other distempers, fancy they have it till they really bring it, and so have it because they fancied they should have it?

Mother. You forgot what I said, son; I said as to our preparations.

Son. You distinguish nicely, madam, but others will take it another way. You say we should always look upon our case as if we really had the distemper; certainly that would be poring too much upon a thing so dreadful! Why, it would make some people go distracted.

Mother. I distinguish clearly, son, though not so nicely as you would have me. I say, as to our preparations, we should do thus, that is to say, we ought to prepare for death as if we had the distemper just now upon us; and my reason is good, because, I can assure you, when the body is agitated with that distemper, there will be as little capacity as there may be time to look up to God and to prepare for death.

Son. Why, madam, you would have us think ourselves all dead men, or as if we were under a sentence of death, only reprieved, *sine die,* a little while, and to be executed at the pleasure of the judge.

Mother. Why, truly our case is no other than that in the whole ordinary course of life; but in this of the plague it is much more so, especially to such whose business and circumstances call them to continue in the city on such an occasion, as you say, son, yours does.

Son. Well, madam, you have been in London during two plagues, that in 1625 and that in 1636, and you are still alive; why may we not fare as well now if it should come?

Mother. The more I have of the mercy of God to account for, child. But I cannot say I was in the city all the while; for the last plague, I was absent in Cheshire; but the first, indeed, I saw wonderful things and terrible to relate; and this makes me say we should all look upon ourselves as dead persons or as reprieved criminals, and giving up ourselves entirely into God's hands, should stand ready expecting to answer at the first call, and say, "Come, Lord Jesus;" for, take my word, son, if it comes you'll say 'tis a time to tremble at, a time to be prepared for, not a time to prepare in.

Son. But, madam, it may please God to avert the judgment; He may be better to us than our fears.

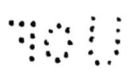

PREPARATIONS FOR THE PLAGUE

Mother. If it should be so, no man would ever repent of his preparations if they were sincere, or say it was so much lost. But flatter not yourself, son, with its not coming; it is not coming, but come. Have you not seen it begun? There are several dead of it already, and more than you think of.

Son. There has one or two died in St. Giles's parish, but it was last December, and we are now in March, and there has been but one more, so that I hope 't is over.

Mother. That hoping 't is over is a snare of the devil; flatter not yourself with it. When the plague begins, though there be one or two that die at first, you never hear it goes off so, it always goes on though it begins slowly, and that slowness of its beginning is what I call the merciful warning given to us all of the approach of the judgment.

Son. So that when one or two die, you would have us take it that the plague is begun?

Mother. Yes, I do insist upon it, and that it always goes on. But farther, let me tell you, I know very well that when our weekly bills set down one or two to die of the plague, you may depend upon there being more, for people are always diligent to conceal their families being infected, because they would not have their shops forsaken, their houses shut up, or themselves be shunned as belonging to infected families; and, therefore, in the last plague of 1636, I remember there was so much fraud used by the parish clerks in forming the weekly bills, that it was certain there died 200 a week of the plague, when by the bills there was only ten, twelve, or fifteen, or thereabouts.

PREPARATIONS FOR THE PLAGUE

Son. So that you look on the plague as a thing already begun among us?

Mother. Indeed, child, I do! and I believe firmly that it is so at this time.

Son. And what would you have us do?

Mother. My answers, son, are short to that question, whether you mean by us, us of this family, or us of the nation. I would have us return to God, lie at His feet, take the words of the Scripture, and say, "Thou hast smitten and Thou wilt bind us up" (Hos. vi. 1). In a word, I would have every one prepare themselves for death; prepare together, and prepare apart.

Son. As much as if they were on their deathbeds?

Mother. Ay, indeed, the very same; and be thankful, humbly thankful for the time allowed for it; thankful that God had in mercy spared them an hour with reserve of health and strength to turn to Him and repent; for then, be assured, when the visitation begins, there will be no room for it, all will be filled with horror and desolation, every one mourning for himself; no composure, no compassion, no affection; no one to comfort, none to assist; nothing but death in all its most dismal shapes, and in its most frightful appearances.

Son. Why, madam, if your rule was to be observed, there would be an immediate cessation of all business, from the king upon the throne to the schoolboy or the beggar in the street; all should fall on their knees together like the people of Nineveh.

Mother. Oh that such a sight was to be seen! I am so fully persuaded that the plague that is coming, and that I say is now begun among us, is a messenger sent from God to scourge us from our crying sins, that if the cry of this nation was as universally sent up to Heaven as was that of the citizens of Nineveh, and with the same sincerity of humiliation, I say, I firmly believe that, as was then the case, God would repent Him of His fierce anger that we perish not.

Son. But you will not see that here, madam.

Mother. No, child, I doubt not, and therefore I am not talking of national humiliations, but of family and personal humiliations and repentance, and that; not on expectation that God should withdraw the judgment from the country wherein we live, but that He should withhold His hand and the hand of His destroying angel from our houses and our families and our persons.

Son. Why, madam, you would put us all into confusion. You would fright and terrify us so that we must shut up our shops, embargo our ships, close our ports; the Custom House would have no business, the Exchange no merchants, the merchandise no market.

Mother. I say again, oh that I could see such a sight in London! It is true it would be as you described it, and indeed it ought to be.

Son. God forbid, madam. Why, we should be all frighted out of our wits.

Mother. Ay, ay, I wish I could see them so out of their wits as that comes to. I should expect that then some miracle of deliverance would follow, as was the case of Nineveh; but it is not to be expected here.

PREPARATIONS FOR THE PLAGUE

Son. No, indeed, madam, I believe not.

Mother. No, no, there is not a spirit of national humiliation among us; but I see national sins rather come up to such a height as they never were at in this nation before. The dregs of the late wars are not purged out, and will not be purged out but by fire, that is to say, by the fire of God's judgment, which is already begun among us.

Son. But they have been as bad formerly, madam.

Mother. They have been as bad formerly, in the revelling days of King ———, but never worse than now, and this even under the pretence of greater reformation; all manner of wickedness and public debauchery being let loose among us, and breaking in upon us like a flood, encouraged even by those who ought to suppress them, and by the example of those from whom we hoped to find examples of good, and at least to have profaneness and immoralities punished and discouraged by them.

Son. The world was always as wicked, I think, as it is now, madam, since I remember it.

Mother. But we hoped this late turn of things would have given a blow to the wickedness of the times, and I think it has rather made them worse.

Son. That lies upon the great men, madam, who should have reformed us, and who should have showed better examples to the people; and you see they have appointed days of humiliation for us. What can they do more?

Mother. Well, and God may visit our magistrates as well as others, but certainly this judgment will fall upon the people too; for though the other are

PREPARATIONS FOR THE PLAGUE

principal, the people are guilty, and 't is from them that God expects a general repentance, and therefore national humiliations are the duty of the people on these occasions.

Son. I see nothing in those public humiliations but formality, and making a kind of holiday of it, a day of idleness and sloth.

Mother. As to that, I hope among serious people it is otherwise, but in the general it is too true, and therefore, to enter no farther into a complaint of what we cannot mend, this, however, we can do: every one can reform for themselves, and repent for themselves; and this is what I would fain see in our family, every one mourning apart.

Son. But even this is not likely to be seen in the manner you would have it.

Mother. No, son, and therefore I am for having everybody prepare for the plague, by preparing for death as seriously and with as much application as if they were actually infected and had the distemper upon them.

Son. Preparations for death, madam? What do you call preparations for death? In the first place, if I am to prepare for death, I must make my will.

Mother. Dear child, do not make a jest of it; I am speaking with a heart full of grief upon a subject which, when it comes, will perhaps be as terrifying to you as to me.

Son. Ay, and more, too, madam. I am not jesting with it, I assure you, but I would hope it may not come; it may please God to prevent it; and

PREPARATIONS FOR THE PLAGUE

therefore I cannot think of such a solemn entering upon preparations for dying, as if it was this minute upon me, for then, as I said, I must make my will, shut up my counting-house, stop all my shipping of goods, put off my servants, and send for the minister, &c.

Mother. This I do really call jesting with it, son; but since you will speak of these things, I must tell you that every man that has any family affairs to settle, ought to do it forthwith; for a time of the plague will be a time for no making of wills and settling estates, I assure you, any more than it will be for repentance; when ministers will not be found to comfort the souls of dying penitents, it may be found still harder to find scriveners to make their wills. When husbands are abandoned of their wives, and wives of their husbands, fathers of their children, and children of their fathers and mothers; when every one flies from one another for fear of their own lives, there will be no room for settling affairs, as you call it.

Son. Dear madam, you make one's blood run chill in the veins to hear you talk so; pray let us talk of somewhat else, this is enough to make one die with the fear of it.

Mother. Oh, child, 't is much worse to die in that condition itself than with the fear of it. I could tell you such stories of the several dreadful circumstances of families and single persons, in the several times of such judgments as these, which have happened in my time, and which I have particularly heard, as would make your blood run chill in your veins indeed.

PREPARATIONS FOR THE PLAGUE

Son. Oh, madam, don't tell us such dismal stories; you should rather encourage us.

Mother. I would say anything to encourage you to go about the preparations that I speak of; but I doubt that is not the encouragement you mean.

Daughter. No, madam, that is not the encouragement my brother means.

Mother. What then, child?

Daughter. My brother thinks you should rather encourage us to hope it will not come, or that if it should, we may escape it.

Mother. What can the end of such encouragement be?

Son. Why, that we should not be always poring upon it, but might live as cheerfully as we used to do.

Daughter. My mother seems to intimate that to encourage us so can have nothing in it but to encourage us to continue unprepared for it.

Son. I hope we are all prepared for it.

Daughter. I can answer but for one; I dare not say I am prepared, unless it be to die at the very thoughts of it.

Son. Ay, why, that's the very thing I say; my mother's enough to fright us all to death.

Mother. Why, as my daughter said, what can I do? To encourage you, as you call it, is to encourage you to put off all preparations. Is it possible for me to do that? No, but I would encourage you to be prepared; that would be to destroy all the reason of fear.

Son. Why, you see my sister says, madam, that she is ready to die at the thoughts of it.

PREPARATIONS FOR THE PLAGUE

Daughter. Oh, but, brother, do not mistake me, 't is not at the thoughts of preparing, but at the thoughts of my not being prepared.

Mother. There is a great deal of difference in that, son.

Son. There is a difference in the cause of the fear, but that frighting of people one way or other is what I cannot think ought to be.

Mother. I cannot think that to move people to prepare themselves for the worst is to fright them; if I was to go to a condemned criminal in Newgate, would it not be my duty to exhort him to prepare for death?

Son. The very comparison is frightful; are we all condemned, then, to die?

Mother. Yes, in the very common notion of life we are all under a sentence; we are all appointed to die, and after death to judgment, only for the present under a merciful reprieve. The comparison may be frightful, but 't is really not so remote from the case; and in the present article of the plague breaking out in a city or town where we live, I think 't is much more to the purpose, and to bid us prepare, I think, is not justly to be called frighting us.

Son. It is alarming us.

Mother. Ay, but, son, it is not alarming us when we ought not to be alarmed, or frighting us without cause.

Son. Well, madam, I will not oppose your cautions. I know you mean well; but you will give us leave to hope that it may not be so bad.

Daughter. Dear brother, I do not find that my

PREPARATIONS FOR THE PLAGUE

mother insists on what will or will not be; but, as the danger at least is real, she moves us to be ready for the worst.

Son. But my mother says the plague is actually begun. I hope not.

Daughter. Well, brother, I hope not too; but I am afraid it is, and from this hour, I assure you, if God please to assist me, I will prepare for it, as if it was not only come and broken out in the city, but come upon me, and I was actually infected with it.

Son. Well, sister, and from this time forward I conclude you will have the plague; nay, you have it already, the very tokens are come out upon you.

[*His sister turns pale and faints away, frighted with his positive telling her she had the plague.*]

Mother. Oh, son, how can you do so? How can you be so cruel to your sister?

Son. Why now, madam, did I not say this was frighting people to death? You see my sister, that I believe is as well prepared as any of us, cannot bear the talking thus.

[*The sister after some little time comes to herself again.*]

Daughter. Oh, brother, how can you talk so?

Son. Why, did you not say you were not frighted at the thoughts of the distemper, but only at your not being prepared for it?

Daughter. Then because I am sensible of my not being prepared for it, I have reason to be surprised at your telling me I had the tokens come out upon me.

Son. Did not my mother tell us we ought all to be told so?

PREPARATIONS FOR THE PLAGUE

Daughter. Dear brother, I am afraid you mistake me and my mother too, though it is frightful to be told so feelingly of the plague, and be bid look upon it as actually begun; yet I cannot say but 't is very necessary we should be so frighted.

Son. Well, sister, then, I have done you no harm in frighting you.

Daughter. No, you have done me no harm; but from this time forward I shall more seriously apply myself to the great work of preparations for death.

Mother. Oh, that the whole nation were so frighted into the same resolution! God assist you, my dear, and cause you to go comfortably in such a work.

Son. You bring it to a more solemn extreme than I intended it, madam. I wish every one may prepare for it, but I cannot say I would have them frighted into their preparations. That was all I meant; and the reason is, because such public alarming the people has in it public mischiefs, it does hurt to the nation in general, injures trade, wounds the poor, sets other nations upon their guard with us as if we were already infected, sinks credit, and discourages the people.

Mother. I have nothing to do with your politics, all your reasons of state are of no weight here; it were better all those mischiefs followed, and the people were prevailed upon to begin a general sincere repentance, than all those things should be avoided, and the poor stupid people be left to sleep in security till they sink into destruction.

Son. Well, madam, that is true too; but these things may be done prudently too, and with respect to the public peace; for all such alarms as disturb

PREPARATIONS FOR THE PLAGUE

people's minds with the fears of public calamities, tend to confusion, and to putting us all in an uproar; as Jonah's preaching to the men of Nineveh that they should be destroyed in forty days, it put all the city into a combustion.

Daughter. And that combustion was the saving the whole city from destruction. Pray, brother, where was the injury done them? they believed the threatening and repented.

Son. Nay, nay, what with the mother and the daughter, you're sure to carry the point. I do not see the case is parallel at all; you do not prophesy that London shall be destroyed.

Daughter. The case differs, indeed, brother, for let what will be said here that the plague is begun, we do not see that the people believe it, or incline to prepare for it; you see how far you are from believing it yourself.

Mother. But, son, to put an end to all the frivolous pleadings about frighting and alarming the people, I say, that to persuade people to preparations for death because such a judgment is likely to come upon them, is not alarming or frighting them at all; a serious persuading men to repent and prepare, is persuading them to put themselves in such a posture as that they may not be frighted, or surprised, or alarmed, for to be prepared is to be past being frighted, and to be in the only condition that gives courage. You may as well say John the Baptist frighted the people when he preached to them, and cried, "Repent, for the kingdom of heaven is at hand."

PREPARATIONS FOR THE PLAGUE

Son. Then we must come, madam, to inquire what you mean by preparations.

Daughter. If I may speak before my mother, I'll tell you, brother, what I believe my mother means, or at least how I understand it.

Mother. I doubt not but you both understand it, and understand it alike.

Daughter. I understand by preparations for death, repentance and a reformed life.

Mother. They are the general, indeed, child; there may be many particulars in them, but I am no preacher, take it there, the rest will follow, of course; repent and reform, those two will contain all the preparations you can want or I desire.

Son. Nobody can object that we ought not to repent and reform.

Mother. Well, child, I only press to the present going about it, because the judgments of God are at hand, and you complain that this is frighting the people, in which I think you are mistaken.

Son. No, madam, if you mean no otherwise, I join with you with all my heart, certainly we should be persuaded by all just and reasonable argument to repentance and reformation. I did not deny that, I only said I hope the plague may not be so near as you fear it is.

Mother. Well, son, we will not differ about that; if it pleases God to spare us, and to spare the land in which we live, I shall be one of the first to rejoice and give thanks; and though I dare not say I expect it, I shall not cease to pray for it, still carrying this along with me in all I have to say of it:

PREPARATIONS FOR THE PLAGUE

that to repent and reform our lives, and turn with all our hearts to the Lord, which is what I mean by preparations, is the only way to be unsurprised at it when it comes upon us. A mind suitably prepared, is a mind fortified and made bold to meet the world; prepared to give up itself into the hands of a merciful Saviour. A heart prepared is the heart the Scripture speaks of when it says, "He shall not be afraid of evil things, whose heart is fixed, trusting in the Lord" (Psalm cxii. 7).

Thus this conference between mother and son ended for that time. It was now about the month of April 1665, and there had died but one of the plague since December, and that was in the beginning of February, so that the eldest brother used frequently to laugh at his sister about the long dialogue they had held with their mother on the subject of the plague coming upon them, and how it was actually begun; and once or twice jested with her a little profanely, as she thought, about her preparations, as she called them, for the plague.

This grieved the young lady, and made her shed tears several times; and once she took the freedom to say: "Dear brother, you jest at my preparations with too much reason, they being but very weak and imperfect. I pray God I may be able to prepare myself better against such a dreadful time, if ever it should come; but I beseech you, brother, to take care that your own preparations be not a jest indeed when such a time comes; and if it should be so, how will you be able to stand it? for certainly nothing but a mind

PREPARATIONS FOR THE PLAGUE

well prepared can be able to bear up. How shall our hearts endure, or our hands be strong, in such a day as that?"

It was in the very anguish of her mind that she did this to her brother, and not with any passion or displeasure at his ill-using her; but she did it with such seriousness, such gravity, and so many tears, that he was very much affected with it, asked her pardon, told her he would not jest with her any more upon that subject, that he was satisfied she was much better prepared than he was, and that she was in the right; that he would for the future do all that lay in his power to encourage her preparations; that though he had not received such impressions himself from his mother's discourse as she had, yet he was far from thinking her in the wrong; and that should such a time come as their mother had talked of, he could not deny but she was much better prepared to stand it than he was; but that his dependence was that God would spare them, and not bring such a calamity upon them.

This healed that little wound his loose way of talking had made, and his sister was pacified. She told him she was glad to find him more serious on a subject so weighty; that as to the freedom he took with her, that was nothing, but that it grieved her so that she could not bear it, to hear him speak slightingly of the most dreadful judgments of God that were at that time abroad in the earth; that she was entirely of her mother's opinion that it would not be long before it broke out here, however he might censure and perhaps ridicule the thought as melancholy

PREPARATIONS FOR THE PLAGUE

and vapourish, and that, as she said, she was fully possessed with a belief of it; so it could not but very sorely afflict her, for his sake, to think how light he made of it; and that her satisfaction was as great, in proportion, to see him abate of the levity with which he had talked of those things.

It was not above a fortnight after this discourse but the town had another alarm, and her brother was the person that brought her home the news of it; for about the 20th of April the news was spread all over the town that the plague was broke out again in St. Giles's parish, and that there was a whole family dead of it.

The young lady was in her chamber one morning when her brother, having been out about his affairs, came home in a very great concern, and coming up to her door, "Oh, sister," says he, "we are all undone." "Undone!" says his sister; "what's the matter?" He could not speak again for a while; but as his sister was frighted, and pressed him again with repeating the words, "What's the matter?" at last he cries out again, "We are all undone, sister. My mother and you were both in the right — the PLAGUE IS BEGUN."

He appeared in the greatest consternation imaginable and his sister had much to do to keep him from swooning. His heart, as he said afterwards, was sunk within him, his thoughts all in confusion, and the affairs both of body and soul lay heavy upon him (for, as I said above, he was a merchant, and engaged in a vast business). His sister received the news without any fright or surprise, but with a calm mind, stood still a while, as it were, musing to bring her mind to a settled frame, while her brother went on with his exclamations. At length, lifting up her eyes and hands, "'Tis the Lord," cries she; "let Him do what seemeth good in His sight;" and immediately applied herself to relieve her brother, and get something for him to take to restore his spirits, comforting him with her words as well as actions.

He was not so overwhelmed but that he could perceive the surprising manner with which his sister, though so young, received the news; and how free from any oppressions or sinking of her spirits; how it did not discompose her, so as to hinder her concern for him. And when he came a little to himself, he said aloud, "Oh, sister! you are happy, that took the early counsel of our dear mother; with what a different courage does a prepared mind receive the impressions of the most dreadful things, from one that, being careless and negligent in these things as I have been, entertains the first thoughts about them, not till they are just upon him."

"Dear brother," says she, "do not talk so of me; my preparations are poor empty things. I have no preparations but these few, an imperfect repentance, and an humble resolution to cast myself upon infinite mercy; and I hope you have gone beyond me in all these, for you have more knowledge, more years, more experience, and more faith too, than I have, or else it is but very weak."

"You are happy, child, let the judgment come when it will," says her brother; "but I have all my work to do. I have had more years and more knowledge, you say; and I must add that I have more work to do, more talents to account for, more misspent time to answer for, and I have made no preparations for this surprising condition we are all like to be in; you know I despised it all."

She had, besides this discourse, inquired of him how things were, and how he understood that, as he called it, the plague was begun. He gave her an account that there had been two men buried in St. Giles-in-the-Fields; that it was true that there was but two put in the weekly bills; but he was assured there were two or three houses infected, and that five people were dead in one, and seven in another, and that the number of burials in St. Giles's parish, which used to be about sixteen or eighteen at most, was now increased to thirty, which intimated strongly that the increase was by the plague, though they concealed it, and put them in of other distempers.

This was a terrifying account, and he was exceedingly affected with it himself, as you see; as for the young lady, his sister, who had long used herself to the thoughts of these things, who expected it to be as it happened, and who, from her mother's discourse, having for some months looked upon the distemper as begun, had seriously applied herself to the great work of preparations for death, and was come to that happy state of being entirely resigned to the disposal of Heaven; this being her case, I say, she was far less surprised with it than her brother, and stood, as it were, ready to submit to the will of God, in whatever way it should please Him to deal with her; and thus she abundantly made good the principle her

PREPARATIONS FOR THE PLAGUE

mother argued upon, viz., that to speak of the plague beforehand as in view, and make preparations for it as a thing certain, was so far from being a needless alarm to the people and frighting and terrifying them, that it was the only way to preserve them; and was the only way to keep the public peace, as he called it, by keeping the people composed and free from the confusions and tumultuous hurries which they are otherwise apt to fall into on such occasions.

But the scene was not, as it were, yet spread, or the tragedy begun; there was another prelude to appear, even in the narrow compass of this one family. Oh, may it not be the case of many among us, upon the present view of things of the like kind.

When the first disorders of the thing were a little abated, and this gentleman come a little more to himself, things took a new turn with him; he was necessarily embarrassed in his business in the day, and in company in the evening; but in the morning had always a little conversation with his sister, and she soon observed that after the first two or three days, in which he continued much affected with the danger they were all in, and his own unprepared condition also, as he owned it to be, — I say, after this she observed that he dropped the discourse by little and little, till at last he said nothing at all of it to her for three or four days. Upon this, one morning as they were talking together, she broke in upon him with it thus: "Dear brother," says she, "you tell me no news now, nor how we stand as to this terrible stroke that is coming upon us; I cannot but be very

PREPARATIONS FOR THE PLAGUE

much concerned to hear what condition we are in; pray how does it go on?"

"God be praised," says he, "the distemper is stopped again. They say it was only a violent fever seized one or two families, and that the people have been in such a fright about it, by the <u>rashness of some old women that set up a cry of the plague</u>, that it has put all the town in an uproar; but 't is stopped, and I saw the weekly bill to-day; the number of burials in St. Giles's are decreased again, and none of the plague or fever more than usual."

Sister. I am glad to hear it, brother; I wish it may hold.

Brother. I hope it will, sister. Come, do not be like my mother.

Sister. I wish I could be like my mother.

Brother. Ay, but do not be like her in this; do not be always foreboding.

Sister. Dear brother, I forebode to nobody but myself. I do not take upon me to teach you, or say anything but just when you ask me.

Brother. Well, but do not forebode to yourself, sister. Why, you will bring yourself to mope, and be dull upon it till you come to have the vapours and be half mad.

Sister. I hope not, brother; I do not think so disconsolately upon it. I hope I am in the hands of God, and 't is my mercy that I am so. I only want more strength to bring my faith to an entire dependence upon Him.

Brother. But still you go upon the old story, that the distemper will certainly come upon us.

[127]

PREPARATIONS FOR THE PLAGUE

Sister. Nay, I cannot but say I expect it as certainly as if it were here just now; that I cannot go from.

Brother. No, no, I hope not. Come, God may be better to us than our fears allow us to suggest; it may go off.

Sister. Then I hope I shall be thankful, but ——

Brother. But what, prithee, girl? Do not be always prophesying evil tidings, that is, ringing knells over us before we are dead.

Sister. Oh dear! how can you talk so, brother? I prophesy nothing. I do not pretend to it, but the thing foretells itself. God has given us notice of it several times, and as good as bid us expect it. Shall I be so blind, and not take the warning? God forbid! Indeed, brother, I cannot help believing that it will certainly come still.

Brother. Well, and is not this, as I say, prophesying evil tidings?

Sister. No, brother, it is not, because I do not trouble anybody with my talk. I should not have said so much to you, but that you extort it. These are notices to myself only.

Brother. But I would have you be encouraged, and have you encourage us all. You are our governess, and when you are dull and melancholy all the family will be so.

Sister. I am not dull and melancholy, but sure, brother, this is not a time to be thoughtless. Nobody can be so that has any common-sense. You was alarmed enough yourself but a week ago. I do not think you have lost those just impressions it made upon you then, though you are not willing they should be seen so plain as they were then.

Brother. It was all without reason, I think verily. I see 't is all nothing but the fright of old women, and of foolish people, worse than old women, that raised the tumult all over the city.

Sister. Well, brother, if it prove so, it will be well; but I am sorry to see you cool so fast upon it, before you are sure the danger is over.

Brother. Child, the danger cannot be said to be over, because it was never a real danger. As an alarm and fright it never had a foundation but in the imagination of a few foolish people, I say, who have so long talked the town into expectation of the plague that, like wildfire, they take at the first touch, and away they run headlong with a story, as if they would have it be so; for fright and wishes equally impose upon people, and make us believe anything. When we either desire to have a thing, or are terribly afraid of it, we believe it at first word, nay, we believe the very rumour of it.

Sister. But you are not sure, brother, that you have been imposed upon in this.

Brother. Yes, very sure, very sure. I am satisfied 't is all a rumour, a mere noise, and there is nothing at all in it but what I tell you.

Sister. You do not know it of your own knowledge, brother?

Brother. I have not been up there indeed, but if you will, I'll go to the very houses and inquire into all the particulars, though I think I am very well informed how it is.

PREPARATIONS FOR THE PLAGUE

Sister. By no means, brother; I would not have you go for a thousand pounds.

Brother. I don't think there is any danger in it at all. I would not value going there a farthing; the people that were sick are in their graves, or well again, and all is over.

Sister. Well, brother, I can say nothing to it, you know those things better than I. However, as you have no occasion to go thither, don't talk of that, I entreat you.

Brother. There is no occasion, indeed, for I am satisfied of the thing, and so is the whole city in general.

Sister. Well, God fit us all for His will, and grant we may be prepared to meet Him with a due submission in all His providences of what kind soever.

Brother. You are mighty solemn, child, about it; 't is strange you cannot be satisfied as other people are. Why, your fright might be over by this time, one would think. Why, 't is almost a fortnight ago.

Sister. Dear brother, I hope I should not be frighted if it were already come; but I desire to be seriously looking up to Heaven for needful courage against the time, for I am fully persuaded it is not far off.

Brother. Well, I see you won't be beaten off of it, you will be prophetic; but if it were to be so, child, we cannot put it off. To what purpose should we anticipate our sorrow and be mourning about it, whether it comes or no?

Sister. Oh, brother, let us remember my mother's words; when it is upon us it will be no time to make our preparations, then the weight will be too heavy,

PREPARATIONS FOR THE PLAGUE

the warning too short. The plague is not a thing that gives warning then, or that gives time for repentance. Now is the time for preparation.

Brother. I hope, my dear, you are thoroughly prepared for it, and therefore do not be dejected, do not be so melancholy. I tell you, child, you must encourage us all.

Sister. No, no, brother, I dare not say I am prepared, and therefore I have cause to be melancholy, as you call it. I have done nothing, and can do nothing but fly to the arms of mercy. Alas! my preparations are poor mean things; you are better prepared than I, to be sure, brother, or else you could not have so much courage. [*Here, as he acknowledged afterward, he was struck with some terrible reflections, and he stood mute for some time; when his sister, who perceived it, went on again.*]

Sister. It is a good thing, brother, to have so much temper in a case of this consequence as you have. I wish I had more courage.

Brother. Well, we will talk of that another time.

[*He could not hold it any longer, but retired.*]

"Well," said he to himself, "this poor child has more religion, ay, and more wisdom too, than all of us. In short, she is seriously preparing for the visitation, should it come; and while I reproach her with being frighted, 't is evident I was more frighted than she was when the alarm of its being broke out last week at St. Giles's run among us; and should it really come upon us, I know not what to say. Her words are very true, 't will be no time for preparation then."

PREPARATIONS FOR THE PLAGUE

The same day, in the evening, being in his counting-house with his brother, he began to talk a little with him about it. "Brother," says he, "I cannot help having some dull thoughts in my head sometimes about this talk that is so public, that we are like to have the plague among us this summer."

2nd Brother. Some dull thoughts, do you call it? I assure you I am almost distracted about it.

1st Brother. It would put our business all into confusion if it should come.

2nd Brother. Into confusion, do you say? nay, it would ruin us all.

1st Brother. No, I hope 't would not ruin us neither.

2nd Brother. It would ruin me, I am sure; my very heart sinks within me when I speak of it.

1st Brother. What do you mean? Why, you are worse than our governess.

2nd Brother. She, poor child! she is in the best case of us all, she is safe, come or not come; I wish I were in her condition, then I could have courage enough.

1st Brother. You mean as to the religious part, I suppose; indeed, she is a serious dear child; I have had a long discourse about it with her; she talks like an angel.

2nd Brother. She has been preparing for this calamity a great while; she is happy; but who can say they have done as she has done?

1st Brother. But hark 'e, you talk as she does in one part; why, you talk as if you were sure we should have it among us; I hope the danger is over.

PREPARATIONS FOR THE PLAGUE

2nd Brother. Over! How can you talk so; I wonder you can be so secure.

1st Brother. Why, what have you heard about it to-day?

2nd Brother. Nay, I have heard nothing to-day; but you know how it is as well as I.

1st Brother. I know there was none in the last week's bill of the plague; and I am told there will be none in this.

2nd Brother. As to the bills, I wonder you should lay any stress upon what they say; you know well enough they are managed not to put them in openly of the plague. Private people get their dead put in of other distempers, that their houses may not be marked or ordered to be shut up; they bribe the searchers and parish officers; and, on the other hand, the public themselves are not willing to have the town alarmed; it would make a terrible alarm all over the world, you know; the ships will be denied product all over the world, and it will ruin trade at home and abroad; but alas! that's a trifle to what I talk of.

1st Brother. Why, you talk as if it was not over indeed; is it really your opinion, then, that it is not over?

2nd Brother. My opinion! Ay, and everybody's opinion, too, besides mine.

1st Brother. Why, by your discourse it is really begun.

2nd Brother. Depend upon it, 't is more than begun, 't is spread every way into several streets in St. Giles's; and they will not be able to conceal it long.

PREPARATIONS FOR THE PLAGUE

1st Brother. You are enough to put the whole town in a fright, brother; why, you are as bad as my sister the governess.

2nd Brother. Would I was as good as my sister. But what do you mean by being as bad as she is? She is frighted at it, I suppose, as I am.

1st Brother. Why, truly I don't know whether she is or no; for when I came about a fortnight ago, and told her the plague was begun, as you know we all heard it was, she received the news with such a composure of mind as, I confess, I wondered at, and after considerable time of silence, answered only that it was the hand of God, and He ought to do as pleases Him with us.

2nd Brother. That was like her, indeed; but don't say I am like her, I do not pretend to it, I assure you; I am all horror and confusion at the thoughts of it.

1st Brother. I do not say you are like her so, indeed I don't know it; but you are like her in this, she is for alarming everybody, as if the plague was actually among us, when she knows nothing of it; and so are you.

2nd Brother. Well, but hark 'e, brother, have a care of being in a worse extreme; for you seem to be for lulling yourself asleep, when you know the flame is kindled.

1st Brother. Do I know it is kindled? Don't say so; I hope 't is not.

2nd Brother. You cannot seriously say you hope it is not; you may say, as I do, that you wish it were not; but you cannot but know it is actually begun, it

PREPARATIONS FOR THE PLAGUE

is spread a great way already, and in a very few weeks will be all over the city.

1st Brother. You make my blood run chill in my veins. What do you mean? I cannot say I know it; I was really of the opinion it was stopped again, and that the danger was over, at least for the present.

2nd Brother. And so your first apprehensions cooled again, I perceive.

1st Brother. That 'twas too much my case, I confess.

2nd Brother. And was mine too, after the first appearance of it at Christmas last. I have been just like a sick-bed penitent — as soon as the fear was over the penitence cooled and abated. But I feel the return with a double reproach upon me. I think it will sink me before the distemper comes.

1st Brother. Well, but do not be so positive. I hope you are not so sure of the bad news as you make yourself.

2nd Brother. Dear brother, why, you and I know how these things are abroad. Don't you know how the plague at Messina came creeping on just when we left the city, and went away again two or three times; but as soon as the sun advanced, and they got into May, it broke out like a fire that had been smothered with hot ashes; and what havoc it made, and the like, at Gallipoli and on the Calabrian Coast? Depend upon it, the distemper is only smothered with these northerly winds, so that it creeps slowly on; but as soon as the winds come westerly, and the weather is a little close and warm, you will see dreadful work here. I do not speak to alarm you, but we should not be blind to our own danger.

PREPARATIONS FOR THE PLAGUE

This discourse ended here for the present; but the very next day, which was about the 3rd or 4th of May, the youngest brother having been out in the morning, and coming into the counting-house where his brother was, wanting very much to give vent to his thoughts, he desired one of their servants who was there to withdraw, and shutting the door after him, his brother was just going to open the door again to go out too, but he said, "Don't go out, brother. I want to speak with you." So his brother sat down, and seeing him look a little disordered, he said, "What's the matter, brother? Have you heard any bad news?"

2nd Brother. Ay, ay, bad news enough, I assure you. We are all undone at last.

1st Brother. What is it? What, do you hear any more of the plague?

2nd Brother. Any more of it! Why, 'tis come into the city. There is one dead in the next street to us almost; 'tis but in Bearbinder Lane.

1st Brother. What! of the plague itself?

2nd Brother. Ay, indeed! My Lord Mayor sent two surgeons to search the body, and they have both given it in that he died of the plague. He was a Frenchman. I told you how it would be.

1st Brother. Well, but this may be some straggling loose fellow that has come down from St. Giles's for fear of it, because it was there about a fortnight ago.

2nd Brother. Don't let us flatter ourselves any longer, brother, or trifle with Heaven. It is spread at the other end of the town into the Strand, and

PREPARATIONS FOR THE PLAGUE

from thence into Holborn. You shall see in two or three weeks more what dreadful work it will make.

1st Brother. What shall we do, brother? What will become of us all, and what will become of the business?

2nd Brother. Nay, what will become of our souls? I am undone if I stay here. I'll go over to France.

1st Brother. Alas! it is too late for that, brother. Before you can get thither their ports will be all locked up. They won't let a vessel from England come near them, you may be sure.

2nd Brother. I am sure it's too late for something else. I have mocked God with that part once already.

1st Brother. You are enough to terrify one to death. Let us see a little about us before we talk thus.

2nd Brother. Oh, brother, you do by the danger as I have done by my preparations — put it off as long as you can. You talk of seeing about us. Why, you will see in a very few days the plague be about us, and no room to escape from it. I warrant you will see people preparing to get out of this dreadful city as fast as they can, if you do go but as far as the Exchange, and all trade in a kind of stagnation, and it is time indeed it should be so.

1st Brother. I do not see that we can go out of it, at least not I, unless I will give up all our business, and leave everything to be ruined, and be a booty for the next comer.

2nd Brother. I am sure if I stay here, I shall look upon myself as a dead man.

1st Brother. I hope not, brother; all do not perish in the worst plague; though the plague were to come, sure it will leave some of us behind.

2nd Brother. But I have no room to expect that I should be kept.

1st Brother. Why not? I hope you will; do not be frighted.

2nd Brother. Oh, I have mocked God, I say, with my former preparations. When I was justly alarmed I pretended repentance and reformation; but when the fright was over, and we flattered ourselves that the destroying angel was passed over, I cooled and abated in my warmth, and became the same loose, wicked fellow I was before. I have broke all my vows and resolutions, dropped my preparations, and how can I go about the same work again now?

1st Brother. I hope it will not be too late; you talk like a distracted man. Why, 'tis never too late to call upon God for mercy.

2nd Brother. No, but it may be too late to obtain it. Besides, when the distemper comes among us, what time, what temper, what power to look up? what capacity to look in? what calling upon God in the agonies of a plague swelling, or in the distraction of the fever? It is too late, brother, it should have been done before; I am almost distracted already with the thoughts of it.

1st Brother. You will distract yourself and me too at this rate; why, what must be done?

2nd Brother. I may well say, "Lord, be merciful to me," for I am at my wits' ends, and know not what to do. I wish you would let us shut up the counting-house, and let us be gone.

PREPARATIONS FOR THE PLAGUE

1st Brother. Be gone; whither shall we go?

2nd Brother. Nay, anywhere. I am sure I shall never be able to stand it; my very heart dies within me at the apprehensions and the fright of it.

1st Brother. But you must endeavour to rouse up your spirits and not be cast down.

2nd Brother. Oh, brother, whose heart can endure, or whose hand be strong in the day that God shall deal with them? God is now taking us all into His own hands; we shall no more be able to dally with Him — repent, and go back, and repent again, and go back again. Oh, 't is dreadful work to make a jest of our repentance as I have done.

1st Brother. I beseech you, brother, compose yourself; you will die with the fright indeed at this rate. Come, I 'll go out and see what I can learn of it, and what measures are to be taken.

Thus this discourse ended also, and the elder brother went out into the city, and he found it to be all true as his brother had said; that the plague now spread into several parishes at the other end of the town, and that there was particularly, in the old place, five or six families infected, that is, at St. Giles's, near Long Acre, and about the north end of Drury Lane; also it spread down Drury Lane into St. Clement's parish, and the other way into St. Andrew's, Holborn; so that it apparently went forward towards the city, and the next weekly bill had nine persons put in of the plague, besides those that were concealed.

The eldest brother came home in the evening, and

PREPARATIONS FOR THE PLAGUE

as he found all that his brother said was true, he was very anxious about it, though he did not discover it so much as his brother; but, in short, the whole house was very melancholy. It is true the younger's melancholy was different from the rest, and very particular, because it was attended with a sadness of another kind — I mean the great concern he was under for his future state.

He had several conversations upon the subject with his brother, which chiefly turned upon the measures that they were to take to preserve themselves, and to put their business in a posture to receive as little damage as possible by so general interruption as it was like to meet with on this occasion; but as these things do not so nearly concern the affair of religious preparations, I have no exact account of them, nor are the particulars of any value in this discourse. This much I learn from what I have collected, namely, that he did not receive any manner of satisfaction or comfort from his eldest brother in the particular thing that afflicted him; and continuing very disconsolate, his pious sister, who was greatly concerned for him, came into his chamber one day, about ten days after the first talk with his brother, where he was sitting very pensive and heavy, and began to comfort him.

Sister. Dear brother, I am very sorry to see you in this melancholy, discouraged condition; what can I do for you? It is a sad time with us all.

Brother. Poor child, thou canst do nothing for me but pray for me; do that, child, however.

PREPARATIONS FOR THE PLAGUE

Sister. I pray for you, brother! that I do always; but what am I that you should ask me to pray for you? Shall I send for some good minister to pray with you, and for you, and to comfort you, that may be of some use to you?

Brother. No, no; come sit down here, thou art a good comforter enough to me. Tell me, my dear, what upholds your mind in this dismal time; for you have the most courage and the most composure of mind, they say, of the whole family?

Sister. No, no, you are quite wrong; my brother outdoes us all, he is like one above it all, that lived unshaken with any apprehensions whatever; he has a strong faith. Oh, that I had a heart so prepared, so steady, so unconcerned as he has.

Brother. Sister, sister, you mistake the point; my brother puts the evil day far from him, buoys himself up with hopes that the judgment will pass over, and that it is not so near or so certain as we have all reason to see it is, and he flatters himself with this, or with escaping it if it comes. I tell you, he has no more courage than other people, but I think he is stupid.

Sister. No, no, my brother is a good man, I hope. He is not so secure in a time of such danger but upon very good ground; he has a perfect calm in his mind for aught I see, sure that can never be but upon a firm dependence upon God. Oh, if I could arrive to that, if it were God's will!

Brother. I am sorry to say, sister, that you are mistaken. He knows nothing of that happy condition

PREPARATIONS FOR THE PLAGUE

you speak of, nor I neither. You are in a better state than any of us.

Sister. Dear brother, do not say so of me; you grieve me extremely. I that am the worst creature alive, what state can I be in? I hope, too, you are wrong in the case of my brother and yourself.

Brother. This is not a time, sister, to flatter or compliment; the judgments of God are coming upon us; what must be done, what is our work, what is our duty?

Sister. We talk of preparations, and some preach early preparations; I know nothing we can do but learn to die at the feet of Christ as miserable penitents; this is all I can come to.

Brother. Oh, sister, if I could do that I should think myself safe.

Sister. He will accept all that come unto God by Him.

Brother. But I should have come before; to talk of it now is to talk nothing. We cannot be said to come now; we do not come, we are driven.

Sister. That's true; but so His goodness is pleased to act with us that He will accept those who are persuaded by the terrors of the Lord as well as those who are drawn by His love.

Brother. There is no sincerity in coming now.

Sister. I hope there is, brother; many a criminal is accepted, even at the place of execution, which may be called driving, as much as anything.

Brother. 'T is hard work to repent under distress, and 't is hard to entertain notions of our own sincerity under such circumstances. How shall I prepare now,

PREPARATIONS FOR THE PLAGUE

that have not gone about it till the judgments of God are upon us, and I am driven to it, as it were, in the terrors of death?

Sister. Do not discourage me, brother; while you discourage yourself the judgment of God is begun, and we are to prepare for it, that is to say, to be ready to meet Him with our souls prostrate at His feet. We are to say, "'T is the Lord, let Him do with us what seems good in His sight;" and this is a work proper to go about even now. I am sure I must go about it now as well as you; I entreat you, do not discourage me, I want all the help to it possible.

Brother. I do not discourage you, sister; you have been beforehand with the work; you have led a life of preparation a great while. I have lost all the time past, and that doubles the work for the time to come.

Sister. I have done nothing, and can do nothing; neither can any of us do anything but submit and be resigned.

Brother. We must submit and be resigned as to God's disposing of us; but I speak of another work, sister, that lies hard and heavy upon my spirits. I have a long misspent life to look back upon, I have an ocean of crimes to launch through, a weight that sinks the soul, and without God's infinite mercy will sink it for ever; what is resigning to God's disposal to this? No man can resign to be eternally lost; no man can say he submits to be rejected of God. I could cheerfully submit to whatever it pleases God to do with me here, whether to die or to live; but I must be pardoned, sin must be done away, or I am lost and undone; it cannot be said I can resign that point.

Sister. No, brother, I do not mean so; we must resign our bodies, but we are allowed to be humbly importunate for the pardon of our sins, the sanctifying our hearts, and the saving our souls; and then we shall do the other with cheerfulness and satisfaction.

Brother. Well, sister, now you come to me; this pardon is not to be obtained but upon a sincere repentance and a firm faith in Christ; and this is the work, I say, I have still to do, and that you have not neglected as I have done.

Sister. Oh, brother, I have done little, I have it every day to do as well as you, and 't is a work must be renewed every day; I desire to be every day applying to it with all my power. I hope you do so too, for we make fresh work for repentance every day.

Brother. It is a dreadful work to have to do at such a time as this.

Sister. But, brother, though the having deferred our repentance to the last gasp be a discouraging thing, and that, as you say, a sick bed or the time of visitation is not a time for it, yet, blessed be God, it is not forbidden then; it does not make our repentance unlawful, it only unfits us for it; neither, as you suggest, does repenting at last make the repentance be less severe; it may indeed render it suspected to ourselves, but it does not follow that it cannot be sincere because it is late.

Brother. It takes away all the comfort of repentance, that I am sure of, and much of the hope of it too.

PREPARATIONS FOR THE PLAGUE

Sister. But not to go about it at all is still worse, brother.

Brother. I know not what to go about, or when to go about it.

Sister. I hope you know, brother, both what to do and when.

Brother. The time is lapsed, death is at the door, what can be done now? It is not, what our particular frame or temper may be just now, but what the main course and tenor of life has been; we are to be judged according to our works.

Sister. 'T is true the evil, I doubt, is at hand, though I know nothing how it is; my brother told me the plague was ceased again, and all was over; but I lay no stress upon that; I desire to be always what I should be if it was upon me particularly.

Brother. Indeed, 't is far from being over, 't is increasing every day, 't is got into three or four parishes the other end of the town, and it spreads this way apace.

Sister. Well, brother, 't is a loud call upon us, to improve the few days we have left.

Brother. I resolve not to lose a moment, but to apply the time that remains, as much as possible; but, alas! what can I do? Is not all a mere farce, a fright? If the sickness should go off I shall be just the same again.

Sister. You pass sentence upon yourself too rashly, brother; you are no more sure you shall do so than you are sure you shall go to heaven.

Brother. I have a sad rule to judge by; I have done so once already, when we had the same apprehensions five months ago, and what can I say less?

I shall be just the same man, for this is all the same thing, 't is being driven into an harbour by a storm; as soon as the storm is over the ship puts to sea again, and goes on the same voyage she was going before, and steers the same course she steered before, and so shall I; I am only driven upon my knees by the storm.

Sister. I hope not, brother. You know the story of the prodigal: he was driven by evident misery and starving, as bad a storm as any man can be driven with; he tells you, "I perish for hunger." He never thought of returning to his father till he was ready to perish, that is, just at the gate of destruction.

Brother. That's but a parable, sister.

Sister. But remember, brother, what the moral of it was, what the design of the story was, and, above all, who told it.

Brother. That's true, but what is that moral to my case?

Sister. Why, brother, He that told that story with His own mouth is the same Father who is to accept of us prodigals; and, I think, He clearly tells us there, that He will receive us, however late, and by whatever necessity or distress we are driven. What else did He tell us that story for?

Brother. That's a comforting application of it indeed, and I think it will hold.

Sister. I hope it is a true application of it, brother; I am glad it seems to be seasonable to your case.

>[*She perceived that his countenance altered, and that he looked more cheerful than he did before.*]

PREPARATIONS FOR THE PLAGUE

Brother. It is so seasonable to me, that nothing can be more; dear sister, you are a healing preacher to me. That very case is my case, and, as you say, our Blessed Lord gives a plain call in it to every distressed prodigal, to come back when he is ready to perish.

Sister. I am no preacher, brother, I am but a girl — a child in these things — but the story of the prodigal came into my head just then. I hope you are no prodigal.

Brother. Yes, yes, I am a prodigal; I have wasted the substance that I have had given me, the time, and talents of health and strength that has been spared me, and now I am just like him, ready to perish; death is at the door; if it came into your head, as you say, without any forethought, it was God's goodness put it into your head, and thought too; it was spoken for me; I will observe it, I will return to my Father, and say, "Father, I have sinned against Heaven and before Thee," &c.

Sister. Blessed be God for the encouragement you have from it. I desire to make the same use of it myself.

> [*Here they were interrupted by the coming of their elder brother, who had been abroad, and came with very bad news to them.*]

Sister. Here's my brother, I hear him ring at the door.

Brother. Well, then, we shall have some further account of things, dreadful news I do not question.

> [*The brother comes in.*]

Sister. Well, brother, you have been at the Exchange I hear; what news have you, how do things go?

1st Brother. Truly, I know not what to say, 't is bad enough, but it is not worse than it was, at least they tell us so; I have the account that will be in to-morrow's weekly bill, it was brought to my Lord Mayor, as, it seems, was ordered every week, before it is printed.

2nd Brother. What! That is, I suppose, that the number may not be made too large in the article of the plague. They may do what they will, but the people will know those things, and if they see any tricks used with them they will think the worse.

1st Brother. How can you suggest such a thing, brother? There is no room for it; the number is known, and everybody is allowed to see it.

Sister. And, pray, how many is it, brother?

1st Brother. Why, the whole number is but seventeen, and there was fourteen last week, so that the number increased is but three, which is no great matter; and 't is all at that end of the town.

2nd Brother. Mark how partial my brother is in his relation. He says there is but seventeen of the plague; but, pray, how many is there of the spotted fever?

1st Brother. Truly, there is a pretty many of that distemper; indeed, I think 't is twenty-three.

2nd Brother. That's part of the cheat I told you of. People conceal the distemper as much as they can, that their customers may not shun their shops; and so they put them in of the spotted fever or anything they can get the searchers to return them of, when they really die of the plague.

PREPARATIONS FOR THE PLAGUE

1st Brother. I can say nothing to that; I take things always for true when authority publishes them.

2nd Brother. I am for being imposed upon by nobody, especially in a case that so nearly touches my life, as this does.

Sister. I think there is not much in it either way; 't is plain the plague is begun, and spreads apace, and it is not much to the purpose how many it increases this week or next, the case will be decided in three or four weeks more beyond all objection.

2nd Brother. Nay, as it is, we see it spreads apace this way.

1st Brother. But it is not come into the city yet, except that one man who died in Bearbinder Lane a month ago.

Sister. Another month or two, brother, will show us a quite different pace, and instead of seventeen or twenty you will see a thousand a week, perhaps more.

1st Brother. God forbid! Sister, I beseech you, do not prophesy evil things.

2nd Brother. Brother, I beseech you, do not flatter yourself. Will you never be alarmed? Do you consider the numbers of people that there are in such a city as this? My sister talks of a thousand a week; if it comes to be a thorough infection, there may be five times so many die in a week, and the whole town may be a mere pest-house and a desolation.

Sister. My brother sees us discouraged; 't is only that he is not willing to have us be too much

PREPARATIONS FOR THE PLAGUE

frighted; but a few weeks will put us all out of doubt.

1st Brother. I do not either alarm you or endeavour to make you secure, but I see you are both resolved to have it be thought worse than it is, and I am for having it called nothing but what it is. So many have died of it last week, and as many more have died of several particular distempers; 't is time to be frighted and hurried when we see it come upon us; I am not for making things worse than they are.

2nd Brother. Well, brother, that is a good way of talking enough to them that are ready and prepared for the worst, as my sister says you are, and I am glad to hear it; but the more unhappy it is for me, my work is yet to do, and I have differing reasons why I am more alarmed than you, for I am utterly unprepared for it, God knows.

Sister. Ay, and I too.

1st Brother. You are enough to terrify any one to death, both of you. If you are unprepared, you must go and prepare, then, if you think fit; for my part, I cannot bear to hear you talk thus.

[*He goes out, and, as they thought, seemed to be angry.*]

2nd Brother. That's very unkind; he seems to triumph over my being unprepared; it is my unhappiness, but it can be nobody's satisfaction, I think.

Sister. My brother can't mean so; however, brother, let us take the hint and set about the work.

Brother. Oh, sister, is it in any one's power to prepare themselves for such a terrible time as this? How is it to be done? and what can we do?

PREPARATIONS FOR THE PLAGUE

Sister. "The preparation of the heart is from the Lord" (Prov. xvi. 1).

Brother. We talk of preparations as if there was a stated settled form of preparing for the plague, which when performed we were ready for it whenever it came. For my part, I know no preparation for the plague but a preparation for death. He that is ready to die is ready to have the plague.

Sister. I understand it so too, exactly.

Brother. Why, then, dear sister, you are of my mind exactly. Will you join then with me and let us set upon the great work as well together as apart? Let us set up our rest for death, that is, that we shall certainly die of this visitation, and endeavour to bring our souls to such a frame as that we may with cheerfulness throw ourselves into the arms of Divine mercy through the merit of Jesus Christ, whenever He shall summon us, be it by this dreadful visitation or by what other providence He thinks fit.

Sister. I am very little able to forward you in such a work; but I will join in anything that I am able, as well with respect to my own part as to anything else we can do together.

Brother. But what do you look upon to be the first work?

Sister. The first thing I can think of is a full resolution, a firm purpose of heart, to forsake all our sins, and to return heartily to God, who we have offended.

Brother. By returning to God I suppose you understand repenting sincerely for all our past sins, mourning unfeignedly over them, and calling upon God for pardon and forgiveness.

PREPARATIONS FOR THE PLAGUE

Sister. I do so; and there is great encouragement for us to do this, in the Scriptures. Hosea vi. 1: "Come, and let us return unto the Lord: for He hath torn, and He will heal us; He hath smitten, and He will bind us up." Isaiah lv. 7: "Let the wicked forsake his way, and the unrighteous man his thoughts: and let him return unto the Lord, and He will have mercy upon him; and to our God, for He will abundantly pardon." Isaiah xix. 22, 25: "And the Lord shall smite Egypt: He shall smite and heal it: and they shall return even to the Lord, and He shall be intreated of them, and shall heal them. Whom the Lord of Hosts shall bless, saying Blessed be Egypt my people, and Assyria the work of my hands, and Israel mine inheritance."

Brother. This is true, but how shall we do this, and who can effectually return to God? 'T is a hard work.

Sister. We must look up to Him for assistance, even in this very work. Lam. v. 21: "Turn thou us, O Lord, unto Thee, and we shall be turned; renew our days as of old." Jer. xxxi. 18: "I have surely heard Ephraim bemoaning himself thus; 'Thou hast chastised me, and I was chastised, as a bullock unaccustomed to the yoke: turn Thou me, and I shall be turned; for Thou art the Lord my God.'" Ezek. xviii. 30: "Repent, and turn yourselves from all your transgressions; so iniquity shall not be your ruin." Verses 31, 32: "Cast away from you all your transgressions, whereby ye have transgressed; and make you a new heart and a new spirit: for why will ye die, O house of Israel? For I have no pleasure in the death of him that dieth, saith the Lord God:

wherefore turn yourselves, and live ye." Ezek. xxxiii. 11: "Say unto them, As I live, saith the Lord God, I have no pleasure in the death of the wicked, but that the wicked turn from his way and live: turn ye, turn ye from your evil ways; for why will ye die, O house of Israel?"

Brother. There is another text which touches my very soul every time I read it; methinks it speaks to me. It is the very sort of turning that I think I want, and it seems to be even a direction to me how to turn, and what turning to God means in His own sense of it; how He is pleased to understand it, or what it is He will accept as a sincere turning to Him; it is in Joel ii. 12, 13: "Therefore also now, saith the Lord, turn ye even to Me with all your heart, and with fasting, and with weeping, and with mourning: and rend your heart, and not your garments, and turn unto the Lord your God: for He is gracious and merciful, slow to anger, and of great kindness, and repenteth Him of the evil."

Sister. That is an extraordinary place, indeed. I had omitted it, but I remember it very well, and the words of the verse before it seem to make the reason for that particular call of turning to God to be much the same with what is before us.

Brother. I did not look at that part. The call was loud to me, and I see reason enough before me; it affected me indeed exceedingly.

Sister. But the words immediately before will add to it still. Pray look here.

[*She turns to the words, and gives him the book, and he reads them.*]

PREPARATIONS FOR THE PLAGUE

Brother. They are wonderful indeed. Verse 11: "For the day of the Lord is great and very terrible. Who can abide it?" Ay, who can abide it? Who indeed can abide it? 'T is our case just now; the judgment that is now coming upon us may well be said to be the day of the Lord, and it is very terrible, indeed none can be able to abide it.

Sister. The next words are ushered in with this as a reason for them, "Therefore turn unto the Lord with all your hearts, with fasting, with weeping, and with mourning."

Brother. Dear sister, this is indeed our direction; let us obey the voice of our rule, and we cannot be wrong in it.

Sister. Nay, they are the words of God Himself, that is to say, the prophet speaks them as immediately from God, and in His very name, "Therefore also now saith the Lord;" and the next words are as if God spoke immediately, "Turn ye even to Me."

Brother. This is a call to us, to me, sister, in particular, and I have great reason for it, and do it in the particular manner directed — namely, with fasting, with weeping, and with mourning.

Sister. 'T is a call to me as well as to you, brother, and I have as much reason to think 't is directed particularly to me as you can have, and more too, much more.

Brother. Dear sister, let us dispute that no longer between us. Will you join with me in this work? Shall we repent together, and humble our souls together?

PREPARATIONS FOR THE PLAGUE

Sister. Ay, brother, with all my heart. I will be thankful to you for so much help in such a work.

Brother. We have opportunity to help and assist one another. God alone knows how long we may be continued together; how long it may be before we may be snatched from one another, or both snatched away, as it were, together.

Sister. I rejoice at the motion, brother; I have had no helps before; I have been alone in all things of this nature; I bless God for the offer, and will join with you in everything that you desire of me, and, above all, in receiving help and counsel and assistance from you.

Here we can follow this happy couple no farther at present, that is, in their particular conversation; but it is to be recorded for the example of others in like case, that they agreed to spend two hours every evening and an hour every morning together in her closet, where they prayed together, read the Scripture together, and discoursed together, as their particular circumstances made it seasonable. In these retirements the brother prayed and made a daily confession of sin, the sister read the Scriptures, and in their discourses they were mutual.

Besides this, they locked themselves up every Tuesday and Friday, and kept the whole day as a solemn fast, neither eating or drinking till about four o'clock in the afternoon; where it might be truly said of them both, as was said of Manasseh, that they humbled themselves greatly before the Lord their God; and as the Scripture above mentioned directed,

PREPARATIONS FOR THE PLAGUE

they did it with fasting and weeping, and with mourning.

The young man in particular was a pattern for penitents, and in an especial manner he was afflicted, and continually reproached himself with having put off his preparation and repentance formerly till the very judgment was at the door, and with having been once before touched with a like sense of the danger, but growing cold and unconcerned again as the danger abated and went off. This robbed him of much of the comfort of his present application, and he continually upbraided himself with it as if it was a test of his future insincerity, and it was very discouraging to him. He would also frequently express himself on that head, how much it should be considered by every one in such cases never to fall back from their own resolutions, and how sad a token it was of real hypocrisy, and particularly how hard it would be for such people, if ever they came to be true penitents, to believe themselves so, or to receive the comfort of their own humiliations.

In this distress of mind he received great assistance from the comforting discourses and excellent example of his pious sister, who was now the companion of his best hours, and his support in his greatest discouragements.

She had given the first life to his resolutions by hinting to him that our blessed Saviour Himself was the author of that parable of the prodigal; and that as it was said, introductory to the parable of the unjust judge, that He speaks a parable to them to this end, that men ought always to pray and not to faint; so

PREPARATIONS FOR THE PLAGUE

that it might be said of the parable of the prodigal, that He spake a parable to this end, that men ought always to return to God their Father when they are in distress, and not to decline for its being late. She had upon all occasions repeated to him such encouraging texts of Scripture as occurred to her to support his resolutions, and that she was daily searching the Bible for such texts of Scripture as might be particularly adapted to these purposes.

It happened that under some of his great discouragements, for he had many, and most of them beginning at the doubts he had upon his mind of his own sincerity, and of his being accepted because of his having not applied himself to his humiliations till it pleased God to bring the terror of the plague upon him, and till the judgment was, as it were, at the door, — I say, under one of the worst dejections, his sister thought of another example. "Come, brother," says she, "I have another Scripture instance for your encouragement, where God accepted one of the worst wretches that ever was alive, and who never returned till he was brought to the greatest extremity — a greater instance of wickedness never was in the world. Nor did he ever think of returning, as we read of, till God struck him, and brought him down to the lowest degree of misery; and yet, upon his humbling himself, he was accepted. Will such an example comfort you?" says she. "I think," says he, "you were born to comfort me. Who was it?" "Here it is," says she. "Take it, as it is recorded on purpose to encourage penitents under the worst circumstances. It is the story of Manasseh, the most wicked of all the kings of God's people (2 Chron. xxxiii.). In the beginning of the chapter to the seventh verse you have an account of his wickedness, such as the like was never in Jerusalem before him, doing abominable things, profaning God's house and His altar, witchcraft, sorcery, and dealing with the devil; also (verse 10), 't is said the Lord spake to him and he would not hearken; so that he resisted even God Himself, and rejected the gracious call of God to him to repent. This, brother, was much worse than what you call growing cold and negligent, and letting your sense of things wear off. Well, after this (verse 11) —'Wherefore the Lord brought upon them the captain of the hosts of the king of Assyria, which took Manasseh among the thorns, and bound him with fetters, and carried him to Babylon.' This was driving him, as you call it, with a witness. He was pulled down from a throne to a dungeon, from a crown of gold and chains of gold as ornaments, to chains of iron to fetter and bind him as one kept for execution. But see verses 12, 13: 'And when he was in affliction, he besought the Lord his God, and humbled himself greatly before the God of his fathers, and prayed unto Him; and He was intreated of him, and heard his supplications, and brought him again to Jerusalem into his own kingdom. Then Manasseh knew that the Lord He was God.' Now, brother," says she, "what think you of all this?" Tears of joy ran down his face while she read the words of the two last verses; and when she asked him at last what he thought of it, "Think of it?" says he. "My dear sister, my happy comforter! I think I will never be discouraged more." And he was in a great degree as good as his word, for he was exceedingly encouraged by it upon all occasions, had recourse to that example when his reflection upon his late repentance gave him any sad thoughts.

But He leaves it as a seasonable caution for us, upon whom the like circumstance of a national visitation seems to be coming, that our preparations may not be adjourned till the judgment is upon us; for that, though it may not be ineffectual through God's mercy for any one to repent then, however late, yet that it will rob us of great comfort, make the danger a thousand times more dreadful, and fill us always with dark and discouraging thoughts, and 't will be very hard to bear up the mind under them.

He warns all men by His own example, that when preparations for death have been put off 't is so much the harder to begin them at all, and the heart once hardened by frequent delaying and putting off is not easily softened to the serious work again, and when it shall at last be brought to go about it heartily it will yet go with a heavy and afflicted mind, and those delays of repentance will be the most abhorred things, [→ Don't delay] even equal to the sins that are to be repented of; that nothing is more certain than that when people put off those preparations to the last, God is often pleased in justice to deny the gift of repentance in their extremity, or, at least, for a great while, and sometimes the comfort of it to the last gasp. But this is a digression. I proceed to the story of the family before me.

These two happy penitents went on in this course

PREPARATIONS FOR THE PLAGUE

for some time. Some short discourses which happened between them, could they have been entirely preserved, might have been very useful to others; the following, however, may not be unprofitable. The brother, it being during one of their private fasts, as above, began thus: —

Brother. Sister, we are under the apprehensions of a terrible judgment, which is already begun, and increases dreadfully among us; pray, let us state between us what is our work upon that account at this time.

Sister. I believe I understand you, brother; you would have us state what we mean by preparations, for these are the things we talk much of, and others, too, when they speak of any serious things; indeed, I have often asked myself what I mean by preparations for the plague.

Brother. Well, and how did you answer your own question?

Sister. Why, I answered as I heard you mention it once to my brother, and I thought you had given a very right account of it, viz., that preparations for the plague were preparations for death, and that they ought to be understood so.

Brother. Well, but the question is much the same then, viz., what is to make preparations for death? or what preparations are proper to be made for death?

Sister. It is a hard question, brother, and requires a better head than mine to give an answer to it.

Brother. But, sister, that which is worse is that the preparations I mean are to be supposed to be made

PREPARATIONS FOR THE PLAGUE

by a man that has been a hardened, extravagant wretch, remarkable for great crimes, &c.

Sister. One that has been old in sin, and that has put off all the calls to repentance, either from conscience or from nature, from reason or from religion, from God or from man.

Brother. Ay, just as I have done, sister.

Sister. No, no, not as you have done, but as you say you have done.

Brother. Well, let that rest; what must such a one do? what must be his preparations?

Sister. The first thing, brother, I think of, is included in that Scripture, Lam. iii. 40: "Let us search and try our ways, and turn again unto the Lord."

Brother. The thing is most apt to the purpose, "search and try our ways," which, as I understand it, is self-examination in the highest extreme.

Sister. Searching, that is, a looking back upon our past life, and into every action of it; not hiding or dropping this search in any particular part that can be brought to memory; not covering any part, but searching ourselves to the bottom.

Brother. And then trying the quality of every action; bringing ourselves to the bar of our consciences, and there impartially subjecting every action of our lives to the judgment of our own reason and conscience; determining, with an unbiassed sincerity, whether such ways and such actions are justifiable at the bar of God or no.

Sister. Blessed be God, there is a bar of conscience, at which we may arraign ourselves, and where, if we

PREPARATIONS FOR THE PLAGUE

try the cause impartially, we may make a right judgment of our actions, and know in what posture we stand.

Brother. But, oh, sister, what is my case? I see beforehand what will be my case. I cannot stand before the judgment-seat of my own heart, how then shall I appear at His enlightened tribunal?

Sister. Do not say you are so, as if none were so but you; I am in the same condition, my own heart condemns me, and God is greater than our hearts. I have nothing to say but this, "Enter not into judgment with Thy servant: for in Thy sight shall no man living be justified" (Psalm cxliii. 2).

Brother. If then we bring our actions to the bar of reason and to the bar of conscience faithfully, we shall see then our state; we shall see what our condition is, and what it will be at the bar of God's judgment.

Sister. Certainly we may.

Brother. Then I must see, and do see, that at that bar I shall be condemned.

Sister. Yes, brother, and I too, and every one, for in His sight shall no man living be justified — in the state as our own actions brought to judgment will appear; but let us go back to the text again, "Let us search and try our ways." What is next?

Brother. It is so, blessed be God; "Let us search and try, and turn again to the Lord;" that is, then, our work at this time.

Sister. Dear brother, our work, in short, is self-examination and repentance; first examination, then humiliation.

PREPARATIONS FOR THE PLAGUE

Brother. It is plain, first search and try our ways, and then turn from them to the Lord; it is taken there as a conclusion that upon searching and trying our ways we shall find they will not bear a trial either at the bar of God or at the bar of conscience, therefore we are to turn from them.

Sister. That is our next work, and how is that to be done?

Brother. That brings us to the other text we had before, Joel ii. 12, 13 — it must be with all our hearts, with fasting, with weeping, and with mourning. How shall we do this, sister?

Sister. Well, brother, let us go on and see the fruit of it too; read the next verse — 13: "And rend your heart, and not your garments, and turn unto the Lord your God: for He is gracious and merciful, slow to anger, and of great kindness, and repenteth Him of the evil."

Brother. Nay, sister, go on with them, verse 14: "Who knoweth if he will return and repent, and leave a blessing behind him." Here's encouragement, sister! Let us set about this work, for "He is gracious and merciful, slow to anger, and of great kindness."

Here is one of their discourses, or at least a part, and herein may be seen something of that true work of preparation for the plague. Let none flatter themselves with less than this: they who pretend to be making preparations for the plague, that is to say, for death, any other way than by searching and trying their ways and turning to the Lord with fast-

PREPARATIONS FOR THE PLAGUE

ing, with weeping, and with mourning, that is to say, with sincere humiliation and repentance, will but mock and deceive themselves, and will find they have made no preparations at all.

I must leave this pious couple now a while as to their retreat, and take them in common in conversation with their brother and the family. The visitation came on, the plague spread dreadfully, death came like an armed man, and swept away the people like an overflowing stream.

It was now five weeks after the last discourse between the two brothers and the sister, and since the two penitents had retired themselves, that the younger brother, having been out in the city, came in again, and found his elder brother talking with his sister. And now his manner of talking was quite changed, his tale was turned, as you shall see.

1st Brother. Oh, brother, why will you venture to go out?

2nd Brother. Out, why, what can be done? we must go out for family necessaries.

1st Brother. We have been greatly overseen in that, not to have a store of provisions in the house, since we are obliged to stay. You know they did quite otherwise at Naples.

2nd Brother. That's true; but it is too late now.

1st Brother. It is not too late for some things, however; we might get a stock of bread and beer into the house, and you see my mother sends us every week fresh provisions from the country sufficient for us in particular.

2nd Brother. She does just now, but it will not be

PREPARATIONS FOR THE PLAGUE

long, no messenger or servant will dare to bring it in a little more time, for the plague increases so much, the other end of the town is a mere desolation with it; it begins to come round us. I hear 't is got over into Southwark this week; six or eight have died on that side already.

1st Brother. Well, what shall we resolve to do? Shall we venture to stay, or shall we lock up our doors and be gone? What say you, sister?

Sister. I am not fit to give my opinion. I see it is like to be a dreadful time; but what you resolve shall determine me; because, as I have undertaken the charge of your house, your measures make staying my duty or not my duty; so you are not to ask my opinion, but to direct me what to do?

1st Brother. Well, but if you were not under the obligation you speak of, child, which you may be sure we would be far from tying you to in such a case as this, what would you do then?

Sister. Why, then, I should properly belong to my mother's family, and I ought to go thither, and then to act as she should direct.

2nd Brother. But tell us what you think of doing now, child?

Sister. You may assure yourself I will do just as you do, I will live and die with you.[1]

1st Brother. This is all nothing; what we do we must do quickly, there's no time for long consultations. If we intend to go away it must be speedily,

---

[1] This she meant for her second brother in particular, because of the work they were engaged in together.

PREPARATIONS FOR THE PLAGUE

or nobody will receive us; nay, we may carry the plague with us, and do ourselves more hurt than good.

2nd Brother. Nay, all the world almost that have anywhere to go are gone already. But have you thought of any place where to go?

1st Brother. No, not I.

Sister. Why, brother, have you made no provision at all for the time of distress?

1st Brother. No, not I, soul nor body. [*At this word he fetched a great sigh, for he spoke it in a kind of secret passion, and broke out into tears after it; but when the agony was a little over he went on.*] Indeed, sister, you have been in the right all along, and my mother too. I have put this evil day off, and flattered myself it would go off. I have seen such things frequently in Italy, and after the first frights the distemper has vanished again. I was indeed alarmed when I came to you there in April, but I found there were some people who, I thought, made worse of it than they need to do, and I dropped all concern about it, nor have I suffered any impressions to be made upon me since.

Sister. I took it otherwise, brother, and I always thought it was another way: that you were fortified by your extraordinary experiences of God's goodness and your faith in Him, and that, I knew, was a good and justifiable foundation for you to be easy and settled in your mind on.

1st Brother. No, no, I am quite unprepared; and that with this aggravation, that I have neglected and slighted all the warnings of its approach; and now it comes on like an overflowing flood, nothing can stand

PREPARATIONS FOR THE PLAGUE

in its way; we shall see the city in a very little time more a mere general grave for all its inhabitants.

2nd Brother. Not all, I hope, brother.

1st Brother. Truly, I believe there will few remain of those that stay here; they that fly in time may indeed be preserved.

2nd Brother. Well, brother, we are all to be directed by you. What shall we do?

1st Brother. Do! I have nothing to say to you but this, do not follow my dreadful example to put off my repentance and preparation upon a wild presumption of escaping the danger, or, indeed, of its being more favourable than it is like to be; lose not an hour, not a moment. I have lost all my time, and now Heaven is just! I not only have no time for it, but I have no temper for it; when the danger is at the door there's no beginning the work, 't is too late then.

2nd Brother. Compose your mind, brother, and look up to Heaven for direction; and if you think of going anywhere for your safety into the country, my sister and I will remain here to look to the house and preserve things.

1st Brother. No, brother, I won't go away for my own safety and leave you exposed to the danger.

2nd Brother. I hope it may please God to preserve us, but, if not, we are in the way of our duty, and may with the more cheerfulness cast ourselves into His arms.

1st Brother. You talk very different, brother, from your discourse a few months ago.

2nd Brother. I have had a long experience of

PREPARATIONS FOR THE PLAGUE

things since that, and particularly of the right He has to dispose of me, and all that belongs to me; it is my part to submit, 't is His part to do whatever He pleases.

1st Brother. I want such a spirit, brother. How did you get it?

2nd Brother. There's the dear instructor, she has been the healing angel. [*Pointing to his sister, who, he said, had been the cause of all the serious things he had done during the whole time.*]

Sister. I entreat you, brother, do not discourage yourself so. I have been capable of nothing, and have done nothing, neither can any of us do anything.

1st Brother. Well, you came in, brother, since I did, what did you hear of the main thing? What condition are we in?

2nd Brother. Worse and worse, the plague advances this way still in a most surprising manner.

1st Brother. Well, what shall we do?

2nd Brother. I scarce know what.

1st Brother. In short, there's nobody left in the city hardly but in by-places, and where people either have had no time to go, as has been our case, or resolve to stay.

2nd Brother. Let us see a little farther, brother; there are but very few dead in the city yet — I think not above fifty or sixty in all.

This discourse being ended, the second brother and sister began to consider that it would be their lot to stay in the city; but being very anxious for their elder brother, they resolved to persuade him to go away, chiefly with respect to the confusion which they found he was in about his eternal state. In the meantime, as they kept up their daily conferences and fasts as before, they were every day more and more encouraged and comforted, being fully given up to the disposing will of Heaven, let it be which way it would, whether for life or death.

But to bring them to this gradually, we must go back to another of their discourses upon this subject in one of their retirements; the brother began the conference upon the subject of the last discourse thus: —

"Dear sister, I thought we brought our last discourse to a very happy point, viz., that after self-examination, searching, and trying our ways, we should turn to the Lord. I have had some difficulties with myself upon this work of turning to God; we resolved it at our last meeting into repentance, and I think that is plain in the text we were upon, 'Turn with fasting and weeping and mourning.' This I take to be repentance; but is there nothing to do beside? Alas, we may weep and mourn, but as that can make no compensation for our sin, we must look farther."

Sister. It is very true, there is more to be done, but the Scripture is full and plain even in that, for the word, "turn to the Lord," implies, in my judgment, flying to Him for pardon. It is true that the manner of applying to God for pardon of our sins is not expressed in the prophecy of Joel, because they were then under the Old Testament dispensation.

PREPARATIONS FOR THE PLAGUE

Brother. That is what my thoughts resolved it into. Now, sister, I bring it to the New Testament, and I was directed, I hope, to that Scripture (Acts xvi. 30), where the jailor says, "Sirs, what must I do to be saved?" The very words were upon my mind before the particular Scripture occurred to my thoughts. What is my next work? What must I do to be saved? And the answer is directed (verse 31): "And they said, Believe on the Lord Jesus Christ, and thou shalt be saved, and thy house."

Sister. It is most certain, brother, that to our repentance, which we have been called to by that text which we discoursed of last, must be joined the gospel direction of believing on the Lord Jesus Christ, and that is the next work for us to examine ourselves about.

Brother. It is plain, sister, from another text (xx. 21): "Repentance toward God, and faith toward our Lord Jesus Christ."

Sister. Dear brother, if we have but these, we have finished our preparations.

Brother. Then we may say, "Come, Lord Jesus, come quickly."

Sister. The next question, then, is to be assured in these two points.

Brother. Dear sister, I have nothing for it but the example of the man in the Gospel (Mark ix. 24): "Lord, I believe; help Thou mine unbelief." And this is the full exercise of my soul; this is what I desire to dedicate the whole remainder of my time to, be it little or much, to obtain a settled dependence upon the merits and purchase of Christ the blessed Saviour of the world.

PREPARATIONS FOR THE PLAGUE

Sister. There's no other comfortable hope, no other rock, no anchor for the soul but this: He is the hope of His people, and their Saviour in the time of trouble. This is a time of trouble; let us not be anxious whether we are spared or not in this time of trouble; that faith which has carried others through the fire and through the water, will carry us through the fire of a disease. What is it to die by this infectious fever, or, being spared a few years more, be carried away by another, or by any grievous distemper?

Brother. The difference is nothing if it be not in things beyond the grave, for the difference of the time here is so little that it is not worth naming, at least when we come into that state we shall esteem it nothing.

Sister. Let us, then, neither wish or fear in the present desolation, but be entirely resigned, giving up ourselves to Him who has said, He careth for us, and has bid us be careful for nothing; this will be a comfortable state.

Brother. Dear sister, I have been debating long with myself about the comfort of our faith, and about a comfortable dependence. And I have been long questioning whether ever I may arrive to the comfort of it or no, whether the joy and peace of believing may ever be my lot; and I have some reason to believe it will not.

Sister. I hope for you that it may; pray do not foreclose yourself.

Brother. I have such a weight upon me of a long series of folly and wickedness, that the more I search and try my ways, the more I see reason to turn to the Lord with weeping and with mourning. And I believe I shall go so to my grave.

Sister. It may be so; but let me add to you, that it does not follow but you may go to heaven, and then all those tears shall be wiped away from your eyes.

Brother. I have sometimes brought it to this, and blessed be God for it, that though repentance and faith be absolutely necessary to our salvation, yet comfort and assurance is not, and then I remember the words of Job, "Though He slay me, yet will I trust in Him."

Sister. This faith is as effectual, though not so comfortable, as the other. This is my case; I know He is able to help and to save to the uttermost, and I desire to lie at His feet and say, as the apostles, "Whither else shall we go?"

Brother. If my faith will support itself thus far, that I can lie down and die at His feet, I will not say 't is all I can desire, but I do say 't is all I can expect; and 't is just with Him if He should deny me even that.

Sister. We cannot promise or propose to ourselves what we shall do when we come to the extremity. Dear brother, this is such a time of trial as we never had before, nor older people than we are. It pleases God we are yet alive; but death is at the door, and we have reason to expect it every moment, and that a terrible death too. Nothing can stand us instead, but an entire dependence upon infinite mercy, through the merits of Jesus Christ.

Brother. I propose nothing to myself but to depend

PREPARATIONS FOR THE PLAGUE

upon Him, and to look to Him for life; for He is the author of eternal salvation to all that believe on Him. I desire to believe in Him and rest on Him. And this is all my preparations for this dreadful time.

Sister. I know no other preparation, and I trust that this preparation will carry us through whatever it shall please God to suffer us to meet with in this dreadful time that is upon us.

For some time both before and after this discourse, the plague violently increasing, their elder brother had been very pressing with them to leave the town and shift all for themselves; but these two well-prepared souls seemed to receive that part of his proposal coldly, and began to look upon themselves as determined for stay, seeing their brother, whose motions they had resolved at first to be guided by, as the head of the family, had not talked of going away till it was almost impracticable to be done. They had made no provision either for leaving the house and family in trust with anybody, or securing what in such cases might be and was fit to be secured. They had provided no country, being, or place to retreat to; the elder brother, indeed, had a house of his own, and an estate with it, as far off as Cheshire. But it was not possible to carry anything of goods or necessaries so far, especially after they had let it alone so to the last; the ordinary carriers ceased going for some time, and, besides all, there was no passing the roads, the towns were all guarded, the passages stopped. And though they had gotten certificates of health from the Lord Mayor, the city began now to be so infected, that nobody would

PREPARATIONS FOR THE PLAGUE

receive them, no inn would lodge them on the way. And these things had made their moving next to impracticable, so, I say, the second brother and his sister concluded they were to stay.

They were, as above, come to a happy and steady calm of mind with respect to the danger of death; besides their private retirement, they went together twice every day, to commit their souls in a more solemn manner into the hands of God. Hitherto the infection had not only been kept out of their house, but out of their neighbourhood; nobody had died or been infected, as they had heard of, in any part of the street where they lived; but as it was now the latter end of July, the city seemed like a place invested and besieged, for though the plague was not so violent within the walls as without, yet it was more or less in most parts of the city.

They had for some time left off to bury the dead in the usual forms, and in the outparts especially, carts were appointed to go through the streets between the hours of twelve and three in the night with a bellman crying, "Bring out your dead!"

It was not till the first week in August that this dreadful sound was heard within the walls; and at first it was principally in those parishes which were next the city walls, on the side of Cripplegate and Bishopsgate; and that week there died of all diseases above 4000.

Their elder brother came in the week before this, in a very great concern, having been at the Custom House or that way, where he had some warehouses of goods, and had met with some frightful things in his way, and finding his brother and sister together, he breaks out in a tone rather of horror than anger.

"Well, brother," says he, "my sister and you may do what you please, but, in short, I can stand it no longer."

2nd Brother. My sister, and I too, are willing to do whatever you direct, brother; but it has been left among us as a thing undetermined so long that I do not see how it can be done now.

Sister. There may be as much danger, brother, in going as in staying; for I believe you have not yet resolved whither to go.

1st Brother. It is true, I have not; I have done by my family as I have done by my soul — let it lie without any concern about it till it is too late.

Sister. I beseech you do not say so; your family indeed may find it too late to stir, but, blessed be the Lord, your soul is in better hands.

1st Brother. I scarce know what hands I am in, I am at my wits' end; I'll take my horse and go to Cheshire.

Sister. That is giving us your order to stay where we are, for you know we cannot travel so far as circumstances now stand, unless we should resolve to lie in the fields and starve, for nobody would take us in.

1st Brother. Why not? you may have certificates of health from the Lord Mayor.

2nd Brother. You have seen accounts, brother, of several families that have been put to all manner of distress upon the roads on this very account; and some are come back again to London, choosing to meet the worst in their own houses, rather than to

PREPARATIONS FOR THE PLAGUE

wander in the fields and roads, where nobody will let them in, or come near them, or let them pass from place to place.

1st Brother. I know not what to do, I must go somewhere. I am not able to stay here, my very blood runs cold in my veins at what I have met with to-day.

Sister. Why will you go out into the streets, brother?

1st Brother. Nay, I do not think to go any more, till I go away for good and all.

2nd Brother. Hitherto, brother, we have been kept; who knows but it may please God to spare us? Let us keep within doors.

1st Brother. How shall we get provisions? My mother's servant that furnishes us now said the last time he came that he was frighted as he came through the Borough, and that he should be afraid to come much oftener.

While they were under these debates, for it held them three or four days, there came a captain of a ship up to the house, whose ship they (the two brothers) were owners of, and had fitted out for a voyage to Genoa and Messina, where their chief dealing lay, and where, it seems, they had lived.

They were upon one of these discourses, it seems, when this captain came into the counting-house for some despatches which he wanted, where he found his chief merchant under great perplexity about the increases of the plague, and he began himself to tell him that he wondered he had not removed his family all this while; upon which the following discourse

PREPARATIONS FOR THE PLAGUE

began between those two only, for the second brother was gone upstairs with his sister.

Capt. Sir, I perceive you are in some perplexity about your family in this dreadful time.

Mer. Indeed, captain, so I am. My brother and sister too, who are our governors, would have had me left them, have removed into the country two months ago, but I laughed at them and slighted it; but now I must own that I wish with all my heart I had done it.

Capt. I warrant you told them how you used to do abroad, where they make light of such things, they are so frequent.

Mer. So I did indeed, and told my brother, I thought he had known better that had lived at Naples, where, they say, there died 20,000 in one day, though, by the way, it was not true.

Capt. But pray, sir, why do you not go away still? This side of the city and the Rotherhithe side of the river is pretty clear yet, you may all go away that way.

Mer. You mistake the case extremely, captain. We may go out of the town several ways still, but there's no stirring anywhere when we are out; there's not a town upon the road will suffer anybody to pass that comes from London, so that it is impossible to travel, we must e'en stay all and die here; I see no remedy. [*Here the captain mused a while and said nothing, which made the merchant go on.*] What makes you seem surprised at that, captain? It cannot be wondered at, nor can we blame the people, for who would venture to lodge a family from London?

PREPARATIONS FOR THE PLAGUE

I mean, what inn would venture it, and have the plague brought among them?

Capt. I was not surprised at that at all, indeed I was not thinking of it; I was at first surprised to think you, sir, that had so much knowledge of these things, should not have made preparations for your family's retreat a great while before it came, for you have had notice that it was coming on above these six months.

Mer. Oh, captain, wonder no more; we have done by the family as we do by our souls, put off the apprehensions, and that puts off the preparations, and now it is upon us, we are all in confusion.

Capt. Well, but that was not what I paused at. I have a proposal in my thoughts that you may, if you please, with God's blessing, convey your family out of the city still, and that to such a distance as you may at least hope to be safe, and you shall meet with no stops upon the road at all, though you travel a great way.

Mer.[1] We will be all greatly obliged to you for such a proposal. Nothing can be more acceptable at a time of such extremity, for we look upon ourselves as all dead bodies.

Capt. I have but one question to ask by way of caution, but if that cannot be answered I can do nothing.

Mer. I believe I can guess at that question, the nature of the thing guides to it, viz., whether we have not the distemper already among us?

[1] The gentleman was exceedingly pleased with the kindness of the proposal.

PREPARATIONS FOR THE PLAGUE

Capt. That is the question indeed, for if that could not be answered, you know nobody could expect to be assisted, neither could anybody assist them, for they would carry death with them wherever they should go.

Mer. Well, you may be assured upon it that we are all of us, blessed be God, servants and all, as free from the infection or from any distemper at present as ever we were in our lives.

Capt. Why, then, sir, the short of the story is this, have not I a ship here in the river? and is she not your own? except a sixteenth, which I have by your friendship, and one-sixteenth my brother, who will consent to whatever will be for your service. Here we have victuals for her for four months for twenty-two men, and have put her upon the Exchange for Genoa, Naples, and Messina; but we have taken in no goods, but some hogsheads of sugar for your own account, and about fifty fodder of lead for ballast, also of your own. Will anybody ship off anything, for all trade is at a stand? Besides, 't is no purpose to go to sea, for no nation in Europe will give us product, or let us so much as come to an anchor in any of their ports.

Mer. You put a new thought into my head, I confess. Why, captain, would you take us on board? → Refuge on a ship.

Capt. Will I take you on board? Is she not your own ship? Is she not fitted out at your expense? You may, and have a right to, command her and turn me ashore if you think fit.

Mer. Well, but are you willing to take us in?

Capt. How can you ask that question, sir? Why else do I make that proposal?

PREPARATIONS FOR THE PLAGUE

Mer. Where does your ship lie now?

Capt. She did lie, sir, at Rotherhithe, in that they call Cherry Garden Hole; but you know you ordered me to fall down to Deptford, and there we ride ready to fall down lower if we see occasion.

Mer. And have you room for us all?

Capt. Sir, we will make room for you as convenient as if it were in your own house.

Mer. Sit down again, captain. Come, I'll propose it to my brother and sister, and hear what they say to it, for I confess your offer comes to me as if it came from Heaven. 'Tis as if it was a voice from above, a message to save us all from the most dreadful condition that ever family was in. I wonder I should never think of it before.

Upon this he called his brother and sister, and gave them an account of the captain's proposal, and of his own opinion on it. They both said the same, that it seemed to be a merciful dispensation of Providence for the deliverance of the whole family, and the second brother and sister received it with acknowledgments suitable to their opinion as such.

In short, the merchant and the captain immediately entered into measures for the putting it into execution; and to this purpose he caused beds and bedding, linen of all sorts, with all kinds of kitchen furniture, and all family necessaries, to be packed up in cases and boxes and bales, as if for the use of passengers, with all their plate and things of value, and had it fetched away by the ship's long-boat, and another boat which they borrowed, for three days together, not suffering the ship's men or any of them

PREPARATIONS FOR THE PLAGUE

to come on shore, but had it all put on board by his own servants. At the same time the merchant caused the ship's bills, which were hung up on the Exchange, intimating she was ready to take in goods for Italy, to be taken down, though, if he had not, there was no great forwardness in any merchants to ship any goods at that time.

All these three days the captain took to lay in a larger store of provisions, and particularly of fresh provisions; and first he dismissed all the men he had hired for the voyage, except those who were already actually on board, who were his chief mate, boatswain, carpenter, and six seamen or foremast men; and these he forbid to set their feet on shore or on board any other ship, on pain of being turned off.

The history of this embarkation, though not material to the subject in hand, I mean as to the religious preparations for the plague, I yet cannot think proper to omit, because it may be a direction for others to take the same happy measures in the like danger, and perhaps with as good success, for this, as you will hear, succeeded very well.

The captain was a good agent victualler. He laid in a double quantity of biscuit, meal, beer, beef, peas, fish, and everything useful in furnishing a ship for a voyage; but that was not all: he put on board a quantity of hay, and bought two cows, making a platform for them in the hold, which had vacancy enough. He bought a great quantity of fowls, and twelve pigs and the like; and, in short, made provision to a profusion; and this he did with such expedition that everything was on board before them.

PREPARATIONS FOR THE PLAGUE

The ship was now fully ready for them to go on board, and the boat was ordered to come up to Tower Wharf, to take in the family as on the Wednesday, when on the Sabbath day, in the afternoon, their sister was taken very ill, which put them all into a terrible fright. She continued exceeding ill, and particularly vomited violently all Monday, and they made no doubt but it was the plague.

She carried it with an extraordinary composure of mind, meekly committing herself into the hands of Him on whose mercy she had so long depended; in a word, she showed eminently the difference between a mind solemnly prepared for death, and which in earnest had long expected it, and a thoughtless, negligent one, who had put the evil day far from him.

However, as her distemper was not the plague, she soon began to mend, her vomiting abated, and she recovered strength; but I mention it to observe the condition of her elder brother upon this occasion. Now, and not till now, he was thoroughly alarmed; he was frighted and terrified before with the danger he was in, but now he looked upon it that God had struck his family, and that they should all die of the plague very quickly.

He got no sleep that night, when in the middle of the night, between twelve and one o'clock, he heard for the first time that dismal cry, "Bring out your dead!" the cart beginning to go through the street where he lived, being the parish of St. Margaret Pattens, that very night. The noise of the bell, the doleful cry of the bellman, and the rumbling of the cart-wheels, you may suppose joined together to pre-

PREPARATIONS FOR THE PLAGUE

sent to his mind the most frightful ideas, especially increased by the apprehensions that the plague was already in his house, and that his own sister might perhaps be to be fetched out by the cart and the bearers the next night or two at farthest.

He got up and went to his brother's chamber, thinking to awaken him and to sit down by his bedside, but was surprised to find nobody in the room, and that the bed was not unmade; in short, his brother was up praying with his sister, and though he believed she had the plague upon her, yet he would not leave her or stir from her but as necessity obliged him, but sat by her comforting and supporting her mind, with the fruit of their former experiences, and reading comforting Scriptures to her. Thus, I say, they were spending the night, when the elder brother calling his brother by name, the servant that attended told him, and he went out to him, and their short and confused discourse was to this purpose:—

1st Brother. Oh, brother, we are all dead corpses! There's a cart gone by that must fetch us all away.

2nd Brother. What, is the dead-cart [*so it was generally called*] come into our lane?

1st Brother. Ay, ay, I hear the bellman's dismal cry.

2nd Brother. Well, God's will be done with us, let us settle our minds on Him. "He shall not be afraid of evil tidings whose heart is fixed, trusting in the Lord."

1st Brother. How can you go into my sister's chamber? You will get the distemper to be sure. Nay, have you not got it already?

PREPARATIONS FOR THE PLAGUE

2nd Brother. I cannot tell how I may fare as to that, it shall be as God please; but I will not leave her while she has life and sense in her; she has been my soul's comforter, and I will never cease comforting her as long as I am able.

1st Brother. Why, you are strangely altered, and comforted indeed, to what you were when you came into the counting-house to me, and was for running away to France.

2nd Brother. Blessed be God, I am altered, and blessed be that dear messenger of God that is now languishing and just entering joyfully into heaven. She has been a thousand times dearer than a sister to me, she has been an angel of God to me. Oh, that I was in her condition as to the soul, though I were in her condition as to the infection too; as to the last, that is the particular hand of God, and it is our duty to submit; blessed be God 't is no token of His displeasure.

1st Brother. How, brother, is it no mark of God's displeasure? I think it is a sore and heavy judgment, and a token of God's vengeance upon the land.

2nd Brother. It is a national judgment, no doubt, and calls for national humiliation; but I do not think it must always be called a token of God's vindictive hand to any particular person, for then nobody could have any hope of being at peace with God that had the distemper, and there's our dear sister, bad as she is, she has a triumphant joy possesses her whole soul in the blessed assurance of her salvation.

1st Brother. I am glad to hear it, but I am very apt to question those who boast of their assurance of heaven; I think they very often prove hypocrites.

2nd Brother. She is too near heaven to be a counterfeit, brother; besides, she is the humblest, most melted penitent that ever you heard of; the sense of God's pardoning mercy has melted her very soul into penitential tears, and those tears have filled her with joy.

1st Brother. You talk upon contraries, you are all mysterious.

2nd Brother. You may call it mysterious if you will, but 't is a blessed truth, though 't is a mysterious thing to those that understand it not. No repentance, no humility, no tears like those that are raised by any humble sense of infinite, undeserved, forgiving grace; and no joy, no satisfaction of the soul, no rejoicing, nay, triumph of soul, like the joy that is founded in sorrow, founded in repentance.

1st Brother. And is my sister come that length? These are sublime things indeed. [*Here he stopped a while, as in some little confusion, and then went on.*] Oh, brother! what have I been doing? I am undone, what shall I do?

2nd Brother. I see, brother, it has pleased God to visit the family; I hope you will be preserved. I beg of you take boat and go immediately on board the ship; take such servants as you think fit, and your little children, and go away, for you will but finish the ruin of the family if you stay, for if you should be struck they are all undone.

1st Brother. I cannot go without you, brother; if you will go with me I will go.

PREPARATIONS FOR THE PLAGUE

2nd Brother. Do not ask me, I cannot leave her; no, I'll live and die with her. I am sure if I had been the first, she would not have left me; besides, brother, it may not be safe for you to have me go, for, to be sure, I have the seeds of the distemper about me by this time.

He had with much ado prevailed on his brother to resolve upon going the next morning, and not to stay for the ship's boat, which was to come for them two days after. When offering to go into his sister's chamber again, the servants met him softly at the door, and told him she was fallen into a sleep, with a little sweat; upon which he retired into his own chamber again. He waited four or five hours, and still his sister slept most sweetly; upon which he lay down upon his own bed in his clothes, and slept several hours more, and still his sister was not waked.

In a word, she slept till near nine o'clock the next morning, when she waked wonderfully refreshed, her distemper quite abated, the fever gone; and, in a word, it appeared that she had not the least symptoms of the infection upon her, to the inexpressible joy of the whole family.

On the day appointed the boat came up, and the eldest brother, with his two children and one maid-servant and a man-servant, went on foot through the street to Galley Quay, where, it being high water, the boat came close to the shore, and they went all away.

The next day, the boat being ordered up again, the second brother, the sister, and another maid-servant, with an ancient woman that was formerly the sister's nurse, went all off in the same manner.

PREPARATIONS FOR THE PLAGUE

When they were all safe on board, the captain asked their leave to bring his own wife and one child, a little boy of five years old, and a maid to be with him also, which they all agreed willingly to; and thus they were all embarked together; this being the first week in August, by which time the burials in the city and suburbs amounted to no less than 4030 in all, of which of the plague 2817.

They left the house fastened up with no soul in it; but left the care of guarding it to the ordinary watch by night, and two poor men, who by turns kept the outer door by day, took in letters, and any such business as in that time of a cessation of all business might happen; these were particularly directed to take in the weekly bill of mortality, which, with all foreign letters, they ordered to be sent weekly to a house at Greenwich, and gave orders at Greenwich to have them brought to the ship's side, after they had been perfumed and sprinkled with vinegar, and then scorched at the fire, as was then the usage.

The ship, as I observed, lay at an anchor a little above Deptford, where they continued about a fortnight longer; but finding by that time the dreadful increase of the plague, and that it came on eastward from the other end of the town, by the north side of the city, into the parishes of Aldgate, Whitechapel, and Stepney, and particularly began to rage in Wapping, and Ratcliff, and even down to Blackwall; also, that some had died of it in Rotherhithe, and in Deptford, they found they should be, as it were, surrounded; so the captain, at their request, weighed and fell down the river, to a place between Blackwall and Woolwich which they call Bugby's Hole, being a secure place for ships to ride in.

The vessel they were in was a ship of force carrying sixteen guns, but could carry twenty-four; so they lived at large and had room enough. The merchant and his family had the great cabin and steerage to themselves, with some cabins built on purpose for his maid-servants and children in the gun-room; an apartment was built up out of the great cabin for his sister, and her nurse and maid and himself and his brother had each of them a large cabin built in the steerage, so the rest of the great cabin was their dining-room. The captain had the round-house and the little room before it, which they call the cuddy, for his family, and the quarter-deck was their parade or walking place, over which the captain had caused an awning to be built, and covered it so close, both top and sides, that it was like a great hall.

They soon found reason also to remove the place appointed for their letters, and ordered them to Woolwich, both the towns of Deptford and Greenwich being sorely visited.

Here they rode with great satisfaction for all the rest of the month of August, when they received the last weekly bill for the said month of August, which amounted to no less than 7496, a frightful number indeed, and which was still dreadfully increasing, almost 2000 that very week, not reckoning such as died in the towns of Deptford and Greenwich.

This put the merchant upon a new proposal to the captain, which was to go quite away to sea; for he was now in such a dreadful consternation on several

PREPARATIONS FOR THE PLAGUE

accounts, that he was altogether as uneasy as he was before he left his house in London.

While they thus lay in Bugby's Hole, the captain and the merchant's second brother, with their boat, had ventured down to Woolwich, that is to say, to the upper end of the town, but did not go on shore, neither were the people of the town at first willing to let them come on shore, not knowing whence they came, or how they fared on board; and they were the more wary because, besides the town of Greenwich, the plague was raging at Blackwall, also in all that part of the country which contained several villages, all in Stepney and Bromley parishes, such as Blackwall, Poplar, Limehouse, Bow, Old Ford, Bethnal Green, Bromley, Mile End; in the former of which parishes, viz., Stepney, including Whitechapel, there died 1026 people that very week, and the next week 1327.

However, they answered their end at Woolwich, which was first to learn that the town was not yet infected, except two houses at a little distance towards Greenwich, where three or four had died; that the market was yet pretty well furnished with provisions; so they got a good woman of the town to buy such provisions for them as they had occasion for, such as fresh butter, some eggs, and a great quantity of garden stuff, such as the season afforded, with apples in abundance; all which was a great relief to them, having been more tied down to salt meats than agreed with them, being so differing from their usual way of living; they got also fresh meat, as veal and pork, and, in a word, were very well stored with refreshments.

PREPARATIONS FOR THE PLAGUE

But by the next market day the plague was so far got into the town that the country-people came but very thin to the market, by which the quantity of provisions was lessened, and not to be easily had; nor did the merchant care to venture the boat on shore any more.

Then the captain made a little voyage in his boat to Barking Creek, intending to go up the said Creek to Barking Market; but was informed by some of the fishermen's smacks which lay at the mouth of the Creek, that the plague was there also; whether true or not they did not stay to inquire, but came back.

When they found this the merchant grew impatient, and, in short, would lie there no longer, so they weighed and went down the river to a place called Greenhithe; but there being no market there, nor any great store of provisions, and the captain thinking their riding there not so safe as lower down, considering how few hands they had on board, he proposed going as low as Gravesend, where, if it happened to over-blow, they might get some men from the shore.

While they were considering this, they called with a speaking-trumpet to the shore for a boat to come on board; accordingly a boat came off, but they would not let them come on board till they had inquired whether the plague was in the town, nor would the fellows come on board till they inquired whence the ship came last; but afterwards, the men in the boat assuring them that the town was in perfect health, and the captain assuring the town boat that they came from Bugby's Hole only, where they had ridden

PREPARATIONS FOR THE PLAGUE

three weeks, that they were all in perfect health, and came down lower because they heard that the plague was at Blackwall and Woolwich,—I say, after this they became better acquainted.

Here also they had news that the plague was at Gravesend, and, as the people said, at Chatham and Rochester; but, it seems, as they were afterwards informed, that news was not true, only that a rumour had spread over the country to that purpose a great while before it was so. However, this altered their resolutions, and they continued for the present where they were. Though this was no market town, yet they got some fresh provisions, and particularly sent a countryman with a little cart and two horses to Dartford, a market town about three miles up the country, and which at that time was free from the infection, and there they stored themselves again fully.

But the merchant was still uneasy, for he could not bear to lie anywhere with the ship if the plague was at any town beyond him; so he made the captain remove the ship again and fall down to Gravesend, and passing the town he came to an anchor below a place which is since called the New Tavern, being as far as the Custom officers would let him pass without clearing.

Here they were told that the town of Gravesend was perfectly clear of the plague; but as they had been told otherwise at Greenwich, he would not suffer the boat to stir on shore or call any boat to come off to them, but made shift with such provisions as they had.

While they rode here they suffered a violent storm

of wind, in which they were in some danger of driving from their anchors and going on shore; and though there was no doubt of saving their lives, yet it put them in a very great fright lest they should be forced from this little sanctuary (the ship) where they had been hitherto so comfortably sheltered.

However, as they rode out the storm with safety, and got over the danger, the captain told his merchant seriously that he thought it was not safe to ride so low with so few hands; that if he was willing to let him go on shore and get three or four good seamen, which he believed might easily be done, he would then clear the ship at the Fort, and fall down into the Hope, or go to the buoy on the Nore, where he thought they might ride as safe as where they did; but, if not, that then it would be a better way to go up to the upper end of Long Reach and ride there, where he believed there lay five or six ships in the same circumstances, and on the same account with themselves.

The merchant was utterly against going on shore at Gravesend, but especially against taking any more seamen on board; but would have had the captain have stood away for Harwich; but upon second thoughts, as it had been said that the plague came over first from Holland, so to go to Harwich would be just to go in the way of it, the packet boats continuing to go and come between that place and Holland; and they did not know but that Harwich might be infected, and then they were left to the wide world.

In short, they agreed at last to come up the river again, not to Greenhithe, where they lay before, but

PREPARATIONS FOR THE PLAGUE

to the upper part of that which they call Long Reach, which is about three miles nearer London than Greenhithe. Here they had very good riding, and safe, though sometimes blustering, weather. Here lay six other vessels, four above them, and two below them, and though they did not go on board one another, yet they soon became acquainted with one another, and conversed with one another upon the particular circumstances of each ship, and the public state of things also; and they found presently that they were all outward-bound ships, but had not their loading fully in; that they were, as it were, embargoed by the general calamity; that the captains had all their families on board, and most of them had other families on board also; and that they had fallen down there for safety from the plague; and it was to their particular satisfaction that they understood they were all very healthy so far, and that there had not the least appearance of illness been among them.

They had not lain here above three days, but the headmost ship, that which lay at the upper end of the Reach, made a signal to the rest, which this ship did not understand. He found that the rest answered it, and he was going to call to the next ship to know the meaning of it, when the headmost ship's boat came off with the ship's mate on board, and, lying upon their oars, they hailed the captain, who answering, the mate told him his captain ordered him to acquaint them that the next day was the day that the six ships had appointed, ever since they rode there in company, to keep as a weekly fast on the

PREPARATIONS FOR THE PLAGUE

Fasted once a week

present sad occasion, in order to beg to God to preserve them from the pestilence, and that they should be glad these would please join with them in it.

Our captain answered in the name of himself and all that were on board his vessel, that they would join in it with all their hearts, and returned thanks to the captain of the first ship for communicating it to him, desiring to know the time they begun and ended. The officer in the boat told them that they begun at eight o'clock, and resolved not to eat or drink till six in the evening. Accordingly they kept a most religious day of fasting and humiliation on board this ship; but having no minister on board, they made it an act of private devotion only, except we shall call it family devotion. The captain and his family kept themselves retired the whole time within the roundhouse, &c., and not one of them was seen all the day.

Our family, of which we are particularly treating, and therefore can call them so, did the like; but the elder brother was still so confused in his thoughts, and had such a reserved melancholy upon him all the time, that he could do little more than read a sermon or two out of a book to his servants, and then retired himself into his particular cabin, where he spent his time as well as he could, but, as he afterwards said, very uncomfortably to himself.

The second brother and the sister joined together in the private devotion of that day, and spent it as they used to do their usual fasts, namely, in reading the Scriptures and private comforting one another,

PREPARATIONS FOR THE PLAGUE

and endeavouring to give themselves up to the disposing of God's good providence, and in praying with one another, of which more by-and-by.

About three days after this, which was the 6th of September 1665, they received the weekly bill of mortality, being from the 29th of August to the 5th of September, in which the number of dead was 8252 for one week only, whereof of the plague and spotted fever 7145. This was a frightful account, and particularly to them; because the gross of the numbers were in the eastern part of the city and in Southwark side, where at first they had been longest without the infection; and, in short, that it seemed to draw apace towards them.

This filled them all with heaviness, and as by the help of speaking-trumpets they now conversed freely with all the other ships, and all those ships with one another, the merchant, whose mind was still uneasy, caused the captain to call with his trumpet to the rest of the ships, and to desire that the captains of all the ships ahead would come to their round-house windows, and that the captains of the two ships astern would come to the forecastle of their ships, for he had something to propose to them for the common good of them all.

Accordingly they came, and the captain in the name of his chief owner, who was on board, told them how dreadfully the plague was increased, and how the weight of it was all at the east part of the town, and particularly that the towns of Greenwich, Woolwich, Blackwall, West Ham, and Barking were all infected, besides other towns on both sides of them which they had had no account of; that, in short, they should be surrounded with it on every side, and should not be able to get provisions on shore without danger of being infected; and that since they were all, blessed be God, in perfect health at present, and while they had sufficient provisions on board, his advice was, that they should join all together, and by consent put out to sea, and sail to such other port in England, or, if need were, in Ireland, where they might be furnished with provisions and ride with safety. That his merchant assured them he would stand by them and assist them if they would agree together to stand by one another; and that as they were seven sail of ships in company all of good force, they should be able to force the people wherever they should come to furnish them with provisions for their money, or to go on shore and dwell at large, as they found convenient, till this terrible judgment should be overpast.

The captains unanimously agreed that it was a very good proposal, and two of them gave a full and free consent immediately; they two having authority enough in themselves, and having none of their owners' families on board, or that, if they had, they heard the offer and consented to it. The other captains answered that they had every one of them several families of their owners and merchants on board, and they would consult with them, and give their answer.

Accordingly, having called their said owners together, and advised about it, some of them agreed to it, and others seemed rather not to be resolute enough than to differ from it, the women being afraid

PREPARATIONS FOR THE PLAGUE

of the sea at that time of the year; however, their debates took up a great deal of time, so that it was never fully agreed to.

In this interval the dreadful height which the plague was come to may be judged of in the following particulars for three weeks only.

Buried in all London and the parts adjacent, within the bills of mortality:—

From 29th August to 5th September	8252
From 5th September to 12th	7690
From 12th to 19th	8297
Total	24,239

And to show how the principal weight of the infection lay at the eastern and southern parts of the city, the following accounts of the burials for the same three weeks in those parts will make it out:—

From 29th August to 5th September in the parishes of Aldgate, Whitechapel, and Stepney	1770
From 5th September to 12th	1754
From 12th September to 19th	1871
Total	5395

In Southwark side:—

From 29th August to 5th September	1374
From 5th September to 12th	1511
From 12th September to 19th	1631
Total	4516

At the same time, within the walls of the city the distemper was most violent too, for notwithstanding the great number of people which were removed from thence, which was judged to be five times as

PREPARATIONS FOR THE PLAGUE

many, in proportion to the numbers of people, as in the outparts, and though in the beginning of August there died more than twice as many in Cripplegate parish only as died in the whole city, viz., from the 1st of August to the 8th —

Buried in Cripplegate parish	691
Buried in the ninety-seven parishes within the city walls	341

on the contrary, in the three weeks above named, the numbers buried within the walls of the city were as follows: —

From 29th August to 5th September	1118
From 5th to the 12th	1154
From 12th to the 19th	1493
Total	3765

Thus that dreadful affair stood at that time, and these three dismal weeks were worn out in consultations and unsteady resolutions, the poor ladies being both afraid to stay and afraid to go away. At length, the 29th of September (Michaelmas Day), they were surprised in the morning early to hear the headmost ship fire five guns, and, looking out, they found she had spread her ancient and pendants, and all looked with a face of joy; this being, indeed, so unusual at a time of distress, they began to call to one another with their speaking-trumpets, to know what the occasion of it was, when they saw a boat come off from the headmost ship to give them an account of things.

Accordingly the boat came on to every ship, and, at a distance, calling to them one by one, as they

PREPARATIONS FOR THE PLAGUE

rowed by, told them that their captain had received the bill of mortality for the last week, and two letters, with an account that the plague was abated in an extraordinary manner, and that the number of burials was decreased near two thousand.

This was matter of joy sufficient, indeed, to them all, and they all fired their guns, and drank to one another's health, as well as they could at a distance; and, in hopes the distemper would go on to abate, they laid aside their thoughts of going all to sea, as they had intended to do.

Nor did their hopes of the gradual abatement of the distemper disappoint them, for the next week after that the bills decreased 740, and the next 652, and the third week 1849, so that the numbers of burials between the 19th of September and the 17th of October were decreased from 8297 to 3219, and from four parishes being clear of the plague to sixteen parishes; and the very next week after it decreased 1413 more, and twenty-six parishes were entirely clear of infection in the city only.

Any one will conclude that from this happy decrease they were greatly encouraged, and indeed they had reason, for notwithstanding the care they had taken, and the happy, retired condition they were in, even, as it were, separated from all mankind, yet it was a very dismal view they had of what might happen to their lot; for they were, as it was, surrounded with the general affliction; not only the city was thus terribly visited, but all the market towns and towns of note on both sides the river, and a great way into the country, were more or less infected; as Romford,

PREPARATIONS FOR THE PLAGUE

[margin note: Market towns infected]

Barking, Grays, and the villages about on the Essex side, and Greenwich, Woolwich, Dartford, Gravesend, and the city of Rochester, with the towns of Strood and Chatham, adjoining on the Kentish side; so that they had but one course to take, which was that which they had been consulting upon, namely, of putting out to sea, and going to the north, round Scotland to Ireland, which was at best a long and, considering it was winter, a dangerous voyage.

But now they were in great hopes of a complete deliverance, for every week, as above, the plague abated, and they began to see the boats pass and repass as usual to and from London, and several vessels loaden with corn from the coast of Kent and Essex went up to market, venturing in hopes of a good price; as also coasting vessels from the coast of Suffolk with butter and cheese came up in considerable numbers; so that trade seemed to be restored, and the people were not so afraid of one another as usual.

However, they continued where they were, all of them, and agreed that they would not suffer any boat to come on board them from any place whatsoever, or any of their company to go on shore or on board any other vessel, till they found things still better. And in this cautious manner they lived out the whole month of November, by which time the distemper was so far abated in London that the burials for the whole week amounted to but 428, whereof of the plague but 210; abundance of parishes entirely clear of the plague, and but 24 dead of it in the whole city.

PREPARATIONS FOR THE PLAGUE

During this happy decrease of the burials, though they kept their resolutions as to the going up to the city, yet they went on shore with their boats frequently to Purfleet and to Greenhithe, and to other unfrequented places, to get fresh provisions, butter, fowls, eggs, and such like; also to a little town called Rainham, to which there is a small creek that their boats could go up in, and where they employed a butcher to kill some sheep on purpose for them, I mean for all the ships, and where they got information how the infection was in the country; where they found that as it was later coming among them there, so it was not so much abated in proportion in the country as in London, and this made them more cautious.

Besides, as they were thinking of going up to London, they were a little alarmed with what might indeed be reasonably expected, namely, that the people flocking on all hands to London by the necessity of business, prospect of gain, or other things, they would come thither too hastily, and catch the distemper before it was quite gone. And indeed so it was, for the very first week of November, when the plague was decreased to 1031 per week, it increased again 400 in one week; and so again in the first and second weeks in December, when it was fallen, as above, to 210, it increased again almost 100.

This made them more cautious, and whereas before they were for coming up in the ships' boats to London, now they altered their measures, and resolved to weigh their anchors and come up in their ships as they were, and come for the first time no farther than to Deptford Reach, where they would continue till they heard how things went.

Accordingly, they weighed from Long Reach, and having good weather, came all together into the lower end of what they call now Limehouse Reach, a little above Deptford; here they came to an anchor, mooring their ships two and two, close aboard one another; whereas they lay before single and separate one from another. And now they began to be better acquainted, to visit one another, and congratulate their deliverance, and be thankful also (that I am to suppose) to their Great Deliverer for their preservation.

While they continued here, the family I am speaking of sent some of their servants to town, to open and air the house, make fires in the rooms, air and warm the beds, dry the linen and the like; and particularly the merchant, the elder brother, who had been acquainted with such things abroad, caused all the hangings in the house to be taken down, and all except tapestry to be burned. The younger brother would have had them only baked or washed in vinegar, and dried very near the fire; but he was positive to have them burned, as what, he said, might retain an infectious air, though they were not sure any such air was in the house.

Thus after almost four months' absence, all things being prepared within doors, and the whole parish which their house stood in having been several weeks free from the plague, they returned to their habitation, sound and in health; their measures for preparation, as well as for preservation, being such as we may justly recommend to the practice of others, if

PREPARATIONS FOR THE PLAGUE

the like visitation should come upon us, as we have but too much reason to fear it may.

But I cannot leave this subject without returning to the blessed couple, the brother and sister, whose preparations for death are as remarkable and exemplary as the preparations of the other were for life; and which, I hope, I may, with more earnestness than ordinary, recommend for the practice of all such who are apprehensive of the same judgment, and who desire to be supported with the same courage and upon the same religious foundation.

From the time that the elder brother, who we call the merchant, accepted the offer of the captain of the ship, they seemed to be entirely passive in the matter of removing or not removing, leaving it wholly to Providence, and their brother's direction only; indeed, they looked upon the captain's unexpected motion for it to be something like a call from Heaven to them to come out of the danger, and therefore when they found that particular in it, which was not related to them at first, they closed willingly with the offer.

While they were in the ship, they continued their particular conversations upon the subject of death, and their fasts twice a week as before, though they had not so good convenience for their retirement. They were composedly cheerful, and as they were fully resigned, and that upon a good and solid foundation, to the dispositions of Providence, so they left all the other things, such as removing from one place to another, down the river and up the river, wholly to the direction of their brother the merchant.

PREPARATIONS FOR THE PLAGUE

This was the sweet and happy consequence of a serious preparation, which I cannot therefore but earnestly recommend to every Christian's consideration, as that alone which will compose them and make them present to themselves in the greatest distress that can be possible to fall upon them, and in all the dangers of a general infection.

It may, on the contrary, be observed of the first brother (though a religious man too in his degree), yet that having put off the evil day, and endeavoured to keep off the apprehensions of it from his mind, he had likewise put off his preparations, as well of one sort as of another, either for soul or body; and what was the consequence? His passions, not his piety, were agitated when the hour came upon him; he was in a continual hurry of mind, and in a terrible fright, even to amazement and discomposure; he thought himself secure nowhere, and he made all their restraints when he was in the ship so much the more severe by his constant uneasiness, lest the infection should reach them. He would not have had the ship have lain at Long Reach, because he heard the plague was at Dartford, though the town of Dartford lay three or four miles off in the country, and up a creek or river which few boats went up or came down, and none near to them, for they lay near a mile below the creek. He was also afraid in the Hope, because he heard it was at Gravesend, though no boat came near them, and he would not let any of the men go on shore, no, not in the marshes where there were no towns, so much as to buy things that they wanted of the farmers. His

PREPARATIONS FOR THE PLAGUE

mind was also full of horror, and when he read the bills of mortality his flesh would tremble, and he would fall into such agonies as can hardly be described. And thus stood the difference between the prepared and the unprepared; let us choose for ourselves! God grant that every sincere Christian may have his eyes up to Him in all such cases, and prepare his mind by a sincere repentance for all their sins, and a resolved and steady giving themselves up to the Divine disposal; then they shall experience that happy truth, that "he shall not be afraid of evil tidings, whose heart is fixed, trusting in the Lord."

THE DUMB PHILOSOPHER; OR, GREAT BRITAIN'S WONDER

PREFACE

THE formality of a preface to this little book might have been very well omitted, if it were not to gratify the curiosity of some inquisitive people, who, I foresee, will be apt to make objections against the reality of the narrative.

Indeed, the public has too often been imposed upon by fictitious stories, and some of a very late date, so that I think myself obliged, by the usual respect which is paid to candid and impartial readers, to acquaint them, by way of introduction, with what they are to expect, and what they may depend upon, and yet with this caution too, that it is an indication of ill nature or ill manners, if not both, to pry into a secret that's industriously concealed.

However, that there may be nothing wanting on my part, I do hereby assure the reader that the papers from whence the following sheets were extracted are now in town, in the custody of a person of unquestionable reputation, who, I'll be bold to say, will not only be ready but proud to produce them upon a good occasion, and that, I think, is as much satisfaction as the nature of this case requires.

As to the performance, it can signify little now to make an apology upon that account, any further than

PREFACE.

this, that, if the reader pleases, he may take notice that what he has now before him was collected from a large bundle of papers, most of which were writ in short-hand, and very ill digested. However, this may be relied upon, that though the language is something altered, and now and then a word thrown in to help the expression, yet strict care has been taken to speak the author's mind, and keep as close as possible to the meaning of the original. For the design, I think there's nothing need be said in vindication of that. Here's a dumb philosopher introduced to a wicked and degenerate generation as a proper emblem of virtue and morality; and if the world could be persuaded to look upon him with candour and impartiality, and then to copy after him, the Editor has gained his end, and would think himself sufficiently recompensed for his present trouble.

The DUMB PHILOSOPHER; or, GREAT BRITAIN'S WONDER

PART I

AMONG the many strange and surprising events that help to fill the accounts of this last century, I know none that merit more an entire credit, or are more fit to be preserved and handed to posterity, than those I am now going to lay before the public.

Dickory Cronke, the subject of the following narrative, was born at a little hamlet, near St. Columb, in Cornwall, on the 29th of May 1660, being the day and year in which King Charles the Second was restored. His parents were of mean extraction, but honest, industrious people, and well beloved in their neighbourhood. His father's chief business was to work at the tin mines; his mother stayed at home to look after the children, of which they had several living at the same time. Our Dickory was the youngest, and being but a sickly child, had always a double portion of her care and tenderness.

It was upwards of three years before it was discovered that he was born dumb, the knowledge of which at first gave his mother great uneasiness, but finding soon after that he had his hearing, and all his other senses to the greatest perfection, her grief began to abate, and she resolved to have him brought up as well as their circumstances and his capacity would permit.

As he grew, notwithstanding his want of speech, he every day gave some instance of a ready genius, and a genius much superior to the country children, insomuch that several gentlemen in the neighbourhood took particular notice of him, and would often call him *Restoration Dick*, and give him money, &c.

When he came to be eight years of age, his mother agreed with a person in the next village to teach him to read and write, both which, in a very short time, he acquired to such perfection, especially the latter, that he not only taught his own brothers and sisters, but likewise several young men and women in the neighbourhood, which often brought him in small sums, which he always laid out in such necessaries as he stood most in need of.

In this state he continued till he was about twenty, and then he began to reflect how scandalous it was for a young man of his age and circumstances to live idle at home, and so resolves to go with his father to the mines, to try if he could get something towards the support of himself and the family; but being of a tender constitution, and often sick, he soon perceived that sort of business was too hard for him, so was forced to return home and continue in his former station; upon which he grew exceeding melancholy, which his mother observing, she comforted him in the best manner she could, telling him that if it should please God to take her away, she had something left in store for him, which would preserve him against public want.

OR, GREAT BRITAIN'S WONDER

This kind assurance from a mother whom he so dearly loved gave him some, though not an entire, satisfaction; however, he resolves to acquiesce under it till Providence should order something for him more to his content and advantage, which, in a short time, happened according to his wish. The manner was thus:—

One Mr. Owen Parry, a Welsh gentleman of good repute, coming from Bristol to Padstow, a little seaport in the county of Cornwall, near the place where Dickory dwelt, and hearing much of this dumb man's perfections, would needs have him sent for; and finding by his significant gestures and all outward appearances that he much exceeded the character that the country gave of him, took a mighty liking to him, insomuch that he told him, if he would go with him into Pembrokeshire, he would be kind to him, and take care of him as long as he lived.

This kind and unexpected offer was so welcome to poor Dickory, that, without any further consideration, he got a pen and ink and wrote a note, and in a very handsome and submissive manner returned him thanks for his favour, assuring him he would do his best to continue and improve it; and that he would be ready to wait upon him whenever he should be pleased to command.

To shorten the account as much as possible, all things were concluded to their mutual satisfaction, and in about a fortnight's time they set forward for Wales, where Dickory, notwithstanding his dumbness, behaved himself with so much diligence and affability, that he not only gained the love of the family where he lived, but of everybody round him.

In this station he continued till the death of his master, which happened about twenty years afterwards; in all which time, as has been confirmed by several of the family, he was never observed to be anyways disguised by drinking, or to be guilty of any of the follies and irregularities incident to servants in gentlemen's houses. On the contrary, when he had any spare time, his constant custom was to retire with some good book into a private place within call, and there employ himself in reading, and then writing down his observations upon what he read.

After the death of his master, whose loss afflicted him to the last degree, one Mrs. Mary Mordant, a gentlewoman of great virtue and piety and a very good fortune, took him into her service, and carried him with her, first to Bath, and then to Bristol, where, after a lingering distemper, which continued for about four years, she died likewise.

Upon the loss of his mistress, Dickory grew again exceeding melancholy and disconsolate; at length, reflecting that death is but a common debt which all mortals owe to nature, and must be paid sooner or later, he became a little better satisfied, and so determines to get together what he had saved in his service, and then to return to his native country, and there finish his life in privacy and retirement.

Having been, as has been mentioned, about twenty-four years a servant, and having, in the interim, received two legacies, viz., one of thirty pounds, left him by his master, and another of fifteen pounds by his mistress, and being always very frugal, he had got by him in the whole upwards of sixty pounds. "This," thinks he, "with prudent management will be enough to support me as long as I live, and so I'll e'en lay aside all thoughts of future business, and make the best of my way to Cornwall, and there find out some safe and solitary retreat, where I may have liberty to meditate and make my melancholy observations upon the several occurrences of human life."

This resolution prevailed so far that no time was let slip to get everything in readiness to go with the first ship. As to his money, he always kept that locked up by him, unless he sometimes lent it to a friend without interest, for he had a mortal hatred to all sorts of usury or extortion. His books, of which he had a considerable quantity, and some of them very good ones, together with his other equipage, he got packed up, that nothing might be wanting against the first opportunity.

In a few days he heard of a vessel bound to Padstow, the very port he wished to go to, being within four or five miles of the place where he was born. When he came thither, which was in less than a week, his first business was to inquire after the state of his family. It was some time before he could get any information of them, until an old man, that knew his father and mother, and remembered they had a son was born dumb, recollected him, and, after a great deal of difficulty, made him understand that all his family except his youngest sister were dead, and that she was a widow, and lived at a little town called St. Helen's [Helland], about ten miles farther in the country.

This doleful news, we must imagine, must be extremely shocking, and add a new sting to his former affliction; and here it was that he began to exercise the philosopher, and to demonstrate himself both a wise and a good man. "All these things," thinks he, "are the will of Providence, and must not be disputed;" and so he bore up under them with an entire resignation, resolving that, as soon as he could find a place where he might deposit his trunk and boxes with safety, he would go to St. Helen's in quest of his sister.

How his sister and he met, and how transported they were to see each other after so long an interval, I think is not very material. It is enough for the present purpose that Dickory soon recollected his sister, and she him; and after a great many endearing tokens of love and tenderness, he wrote to her, telling her that he believed Providence had bestowed on him as much as would support him as long as he lived, and that if she thought proper he would come and spend the remainder of his days with her.

The good woman no sooner read his proposal than she accepted it, adding, withal, that she could wish her entertainment was better; but, if he would accept of it as it was, she would do her best to make everything easy, and that he should be welcome, upon his own terms, to stay with her as long as he pleased.

This affair being so happily settled to his full satisfaction, he returns to Padstow, to fetch the things he had left behind him, and the next day came back to St. Helen's, where, according to his own proposal, he continued to the day of his death, which happened upon the 29th of May 1718, about the same hour in which he was born.

Having thus given a short detail of the several periods of his life, extracted chiefly from the papers which he left behind him, I come in the next place to make a few observations how he managed himself and spent his time toward the latter part of it.

His constant practice, both winter and summer, was to rise and set with the sun; and, if the weather would permit, he never failed to walk in some unfrequented place for three hours, both morning and evening, and there, it is supposed, he composed the following meditations. The chief part of his sustenance was milk, with a little bread boiled in it, of which, in a morning, after his walk, he would eat the quantity of a pint, and sometimes more. Dinners, he never ate any; and at night he would only have a pretty large piece of bread, and drink a draught of good spring water; and after this method he lived during the whole time he was at St. Helen's. It is observed of him that he never slept out of a bed, nor never lay awake in one; which I take to be an argument, not only of a strong and healthful constitution, but of a mind composed and calm, and entirely free from the ordinary disturbances of human life. He never gave the least signs of complaint or dissatisfaction at anything, unless it was when he heard the tinners swear, or saw them drunk; and then, too, he would get out of the way as soon as he had let them see, by some significant signs, how scandalous and ridiculous they made themselves; and against the next time he met them, would be sure to have a paper ready written, wherein he would represent the folly of drunkenness, and the dangerous consequences that generally attended it.

Idleness was his utter aversion, and if at any time he had finished the business of the day, and was grown weary of reading and writing, in which he daily spent six hours at least, he would certainly find something, either within doors or without, to employ himself.

Much might be said both with regard to the wise and regular management and the prudent methods he took to spend his time well towards the declension of his life; but, as his history may perhaps be shortly published at large by a better hand, I shall only observe in the general that he was a person of great wisdom and sagacity. He understood nature beyond the ordinary capacity, and if he had had a competency of learning suitable to his genius, neither this nor the former ages would have produced a better philosopher or a greater man.

I come next to speak of the manner of his death and the consequences thereof, which are, indeed, very surprising, and, perhaps, not altogether unworthy a general observation. I shall relate them as briefly as I can, and leave every one to believe or disbelieve as he thinks proper.

Upon the 26th of May, 1718, according to his usual method, about four in the afternoon he went out to take his evening walk; but before he could reach the place he intended he was seized with an apoplectic fit, which only gave him liberty to sit down under a tree, where, in an instant, he was deprived of all manner of sense and motion, and so he continued, as appears by his own confession afterwards, for more than fourteen hours.

His sister, who knew how exact he was in all his methods, finding him stay a considerable time beyond the usual hour, concludes that some misfortune must needs have happened to him, or he would certainly have been at home before. In short, she went immediately to all the places he was wont to frequent, but nothing could be heard or seen of him till the next morning, when a young man as he was going to work discovered him, and went home and told his sister that her brother lay in such a place, under a tree, and, as he believed, had been robbed and murdered.

The poor woman, who had all night been under the most dreadful apprehensions, was now frighted and confounded to the last degree. However, recollecting herself, and finding there was no remedy, she got two or three of her neighbours to bear her company, and so hastened with the young man to the tree, where she found her brother lying in the same posture that he had described.

The dismal object at first view startled and surprised everybody present, and filled them full of different notions and conjectures. But some of the company going nearer to him, and finding that he had lost nothing, and that there were no marks of any violence to be discovered about him, they conclude that it must be an apoplectic or some other sudden fit that had surprised him in his walk; upon which his sister and the rest began to feel his hands and face, and observing that he was still warm, and that there were some symptoms of life yet remaining, they conclude that the best way was to carry him home to bed, which was accordingly done with the utmost expedition.

When they had got him into the bed, nothing was omitted that they could think of to bring him to himself, but still he continued utterly insensible for about six hours. At the sixth hour's end he began to move a little, and in a very short time was so far recovered, to the great astonishment of everybody about him, that he was able to look up, and to make a sign to his sister to bring him a cup of water.

After he had drunk the water he soon perceived that all his faculties were returned to their former stations, and though his strength was very much abated by the length and rigour of the fit, yet his intellects were as strong and vigorous as ever.

His sister observing him to look earnestly upon the company, as if he had something extraordinary to communicate to them, fetched him a pen and ink and a sheet of paper, which, after a short pause, he took, and wrote as follows: —

"DEAR SISTER, — I have now no need of pen, ink, and paper, to tell you my meaning. I find the strings that bound up my tongue, and hindered me from speaking, are unloosed, and I have words to express myself as freely and distinctly as any other person. From whence this strange and unexpected event should proceed, I must not pretend to say, any further than this, that 't is doubtless the hand of Providence that has done it, and in that I ought to acquiesce. Pray let me be alone for two or three hours, that I may be at liberty to compose myself, and put my thoughts in the best order I can before I leave them behind me."

The poor woman, though extremely startled at what her brother had written, yet took care to conceal it from the neighbours, who, she knew, as well as she, must be mightily surprised at a thing so utterly unexpected. Says she, "My brother desires to be alone; I believe he may have something in his mind that disturbs him." Upon which the neighbours took their leave and returned home, and his sister shut the door, and left him alone to his private contemplations.

After the company were withdrawn he fell into a sound sleep, which lasted from two till six, and his sister, being apprehensive of the return of his fit, came to the bedside, and asking softly if he wanted anything, he turned about to her and spoke to this effect: "Dear sister, you see me not only recovered out of a terrible fit, but likewise that I have the liberty of speech, a blessing that I have been deprived of almost sixty years, and I am satisfied you are sincerely joyful to find me in the state I now am in; but, alas! 'tis but a mistaken kindness. These are things but of short duration, and if they were to continue for a hundred years longer, I can't see how I should be anyways the better.

"I know the world too well to be fond of it, and am fully satisfied that the difference between a long and a short life is insignificant, especially when I consider the accidents and company I am to encounter.

THE DUMB PHILOSOPHER;

Do but look seriously and impartially upon the astonishing notion of time and eternity, what an immense deal has run out already, and how infinite 't is still in the future; do but seriously and deliberately consider this, and you'll find, upon the whole, that three days and three ages of life come much to the same measure and reckoning."

As soon as he had ended his discourse upon the vanity and uncertainty of human life, he looked steadfastly upon her. "Sister," says he, "I conjure you not to be disturbed at what I am going to tell you, which you will undoubtedly find to be true in every particular. I perceive my glass is run, and I have now no more to do in this world but to take my leave of it; for to-morrow about this time my speech will be again taken from me, and, in a short time, my fit will return; and the next day, which I understand is the day on which I came into this troublesome world, I shall exchange it for another, where, for the future, I shall for ever be free from all manner of sin and sufferings."

The good woman would have made him a reply, but he prevented her by telling her he had no time to hearken to unnecessary complaints or animadversions. "I have a great many things in my mind," says he, "that require a speedy and serious consideration. The time I have to stay is but short, and I have a great deal of important business to do in it. Time and death are both in my view, and seem both to call aloud to me to make no delay. I beg of you, therefore, not to disquiet yourself or me. What must be, must be. The decrees of Providence are eternal and unalterable; why, then, should we torment ourselves about that which we cannot remedy?

"I must confess, my dear sister, I owe you many obligations for your exemplary fondness to me, and do solemnly assure you I shall retain the sense of them to the last moment. All that I have to request of you is, that I may be alone for this night. I have it in my thoughts to leave some short observations behind me, and likewise to discover some things of great weight which have been revealed to me, which may perhaps be of some use hereafter to you and your friends. What credit they may meet with I can't say, but, depend, the consequence, according to their respective periods, will account for them, and vindicate them against the supposition of falsity and mere suggestion."

Upon this, his sister left him till about four in the morning, when coming to his bedside to know if he wanted anything, and how he had rested, he made her this answer: "I have been taking a cursory view of my life, and though I find myself exceedingly deficient in several particulars, yet I bless God I cannot find I have any just grounds to suspect my pardon. In short," says he, "I have spent this night with more inward pleasure and true satisfaction than ever I spent a night through the whole course of my life."

After he had concluded what he had to say upon the satisfaction that attended an innocent and well-spent life, and observed what a mighty consolation it was to persons, not only under the apprehension, but even in the very agonies, of death itself, he desired her to bring him his usual cup of water, and then to help him on with his clothes, that he might sit up, and so be in a better posture to take his leave of her and her friends.

When she had taken him up and placed him at a table where he usually sat, he desired her to bring him his box of papers, and after he had collected those he intended should be preserved, he ordered her to bring a candle, that he might see the rest burnt. The good woman seemed at first to oppose the burning of his papers, till he told her they were only useless trifles, some unfinished observations which he had made in his youthful days, and were not fit to be seen by her or anybody that should come after him.

After he had seen his papers burnt, and placed the rest in their proper order, and had likewise settled all his other affairs, which was only fit to be done between himself and his sister, he desired her to call two or three of the most reputable neighbours, not only to be witnesses of his will, but likewise to hear what he had further to communicate before the return of his fit, which he expected very speedily.

His sister, who had beforehand acquainted two or three of her confidants with all that had happened, was very much rejoiced to hear her brother make so unexpected a concession; and accordingly, without any delay or hesitation, went directly into the neighbourhood and brought home her two select friends, upon whose secrecy and sincerity she knew she might depend upon all accounts.

In her absence he felt several symptoms of the

approach of his fit, which made him a little uneasy, lest it should entirely seize him before he had perfected his will, but that apprehension was quickly removed by her speedy return. After she had introduced her friends into his chamber, he proceeded to express himself in the following manner: —

"Dear sister, you now see your brother upon the brink of eternity; and as the words of dying persons are commonly the most regarded, and make deepest impressions, I cannot suspect but you will suffer the few I am about to say to have always some place in your thoughts, that they may be ready for you to make use of upon any occasion.

"Do not be fond of anything on this side of eternity, or suffer your interest to incline you to break your word, quit your modesty, or to do anything that will not bear the light, and look the world in the face. For be assured of this: the person that values the virtue of his mind and the dignity of his reason, is always easy and well fortified both against death and misfortune, and is perfectly indifferent about the length or shortness of his life. Such a one is solicitous about nothing but his own conduct, and for fear he should be deficient in the duties of religion, and the respective functions of reason and prudence.

"Always go the nearest way to work. Now, the nearest way through all the business of human life are the paths of religion and honesty, and keeping those as directly as you can, you avoid all the dangerous precipices that often lie in the road, and sometimes block up the passage entirely.

THE DUMB PHILOSOPHER;

"Remember that life was but lent at first, and that the remainder is more than you have reason to expect, and consequently ought to be managed with more than ordinary diligence. A wise man spends every day as if it were his last; his hour-glass is always in his hand, and he is never guilty of sluggishness or insincerity."

He was about to proceed when a sudden symptom of the return of his fit put him in mind that it was time to get his will witnessed, which was no sooner done but he took it up and gave it to his sister, telling her that though all he had was hers of right, yet he thought it proper, to prevent even a possibility of a dispute, to write down his mind in the nature of a will, "wherein I have given you," says he, "the little that I have left, except my books and papers, which, as soon as I am dead, I desire may be delivered to Mr. Anthony Barlow, a near relation of my worthy master, Mr. Owen Parry."

This Mr. Anthony Barlow was an old contemplative Welsh gentleman, who, being under some difficulties in his own country, was forced to come into Cornwall and take sanctuary among the tinners. Dickory, though he kept himself as retired as possible, happened to meet him one day upon his walks, and presently remembered that he was the very person that used frequently to come to visit his master while he lived in Pembrokeshire, and so went to him, and by signs made him understand who he was.

The old gentleman, though at first surprised at this unexpected interview, soon recollected that he had formerly seen at Mr. Parry's a dumb man, whom they used to call the Dumb Philosopher, so concludes immediately that consequently this must be he. In short, they soon made themselves known to each other, and from that time contracted a strict friendship and a correspondence by letters, which for the future they mutually managed with the greatest exactness and familiarity.

But to leave this as a matter not much material, and to return to our narrative. By this time Dickory's speech began to falter, which his sister observing, put him in mind that he would do well to make some declaration of his faith and principles of religion, because some reflections had been made upon him upon the account of his neglect, or rather his refusal, to appear at any place of public worship.

"Dear sister," says he, "you observe very well, and I wish the continuance of my speech for a few moments that I might make an ample declaration upon that account. But I find that cannot be; my speech is leaving me so fast that I can only tell you that I have always lived, and now die, an unworthy member of the ancient Catholic and Apostolic Church; and as to my faith and principles, I refer you to my papers, which, I hope, will in some measure vindicate me against the reflections you mention."

He had hardly finished his discourse to his sister and her two friends, and given some short directions relating to his burial, but his speech left him; and what makes the thing the more remarkable, it went away, in all appearance, without giving him any sort of pain or uneasiness.

When he perceived that his speech was entirely

vanished, and that he was again in his original state of dumbness, he took his pen as formerly, and wrote to his sister, signifying that whereas the sudden loss of his speech had deprived him of the opportunity to speak to her and her friends what he intended, he would leave it for them in writing; and so desired he might not be disturbed till the return of his fit, which he expected in six hours at farthest. According to his desire they all left him, and then, with the greatest resignation imaginable, he wrote down the meditations following: —

PART II

An Abstract of his Faith and the Principles of his Religion, &c., which begins thus:

DEAR SISTER, — I thank you for putting me in mind to make a declaration of my faith and the principles of my religion. I find, as you very well observe, I have been under some reflections upon that account, and therefore I think it highly requisite that I set that matter right in the first place. To begin, therefore, with my faith, in which I intend to be as short and as comprehensive as I can:

1. I most firmly believe that it was the eternal will of God, and the result of His infinite wisdom, to create a world, and for the glory of His Majesty to make several sorts of creatures in order and degree one after another: that is to say, angels, or pure immortal spirits; men, consisting of immortal spirits and matter, having rational and sensitive souls;

brutes, having mortal and sensitive souls; and mere vegetatives, such as trees, plants, &c.; and these creatures so made do, as it were, clasp the higher and lower world together.

2. I believe the Holy Scriptures, and everything therein contained, to be the pure and essential word of God; and that, according to these sacred writings, man, the lord and prince of the creation, by his disobedience in Paradise, forfeited his innocence and the dignity of his nature, and subjected himself and all his posterity to sin and misery.

3. I believe, and am fully and entirely satisfied, that God the Father, out of His infinite goodness and compassion to mankind, was pleased to send His only Son, the second person in the holy and undivided Trinity, to mediate for him, and to procure his redemption and eternal salvation.

4. I believe that God the Son, out of His infinite love, and for the glory of the Deity, was pleased voluntarily and freely to descend from heaven, and to take our nature upon Him, and to lead an exemplary life of purity, holiness, and perfect obedience, and at last to suffer an ignominious death upon the cross for the sins of the whole world, and to rise again the third day for our justification.

5. I believe that the Holy Ghost, out of His infinite goodness, was pleased to undertake the office of sanctifying us with His divine grace, and thereby assisting us with faith to believe, will to desire, and power to do all those things that are required of us in this world, in order to entitle us to the blessings of just men made perfect in the world to come.

6. I believe that these three persons are of equal power, majesty, and duration, and that the Godhead of the Father, of the Son, and of the Holy Ghost is all one, and that they are equally uncreate, incomprehensible, eternal, and almighty; and that none is greater or less than the other, but that every one hath one and the same Divine nature and perfections.

These, sister, are the doctrines which have been received and practised by the best men of every age, from the beginning of the Christian religion to this day, and it is upon this I ground my faith and hopes of salvation, not doubting but, if my life and practice have been answerable to them, that I shall be quickly translated out of this kingdom of darkness, out of this world of sorrow, vexation, and confusion, into that blessed kingdom, where I shall cease to grieve and to suffer, and shall be happy to all eternity.

As to my principles in religion, to be as brief as I can, I declare myself to be a member of Christ's Church, which I take to be a universal society of all Christian people, distributed under lawful governors and pastors into particular churches, holding communion with each other in all the essentials of the Christian faith, worship, and discipline; and among these I look upon the Church of England to be the chief and best constituted.

The Church of England is doubtless the great bulwark of the ancient Catholic or Apostolic faith all over the world; a Church that has all the spiritual advantages that the nature of a Church is capable of. From the doctrine and principles of the Church of

England we are taught loyalty to our prince, fidelity to our country, and justice to all mankind: and therefore, as I look upon this to be one of the most excellent branches of the Church Universal, and stands, as it were, between superstition and hypocrisy, I therefore declare, for the satisfaction of you and your friends, as I have always lived so I now die, a true and sincere, though a most unworthy, member of it. And as to my discontinuance of my attendance at the public worship, I refer you to my papers, which I have left with my worthy friend, Mr. Barlow. And thus, my dear sister, I have given you a short account of my faith and the principles of my religion. I come, in the next place, to lay before you a few meditations and observations I have at several times collected together, more particularly those since my retirement to St. Helen's.

Meditations and Observations relating to the Conduct of Human Life in general.

1. Remember how often you have neglected the great duties of religion and virtue, and slighted the opportunities that Providence has put into your hands, and, withal, that you have a set period assigned you for the management of the affairs of human life; and then reflect seriously that, unless you resolve immediately to improve the little remains, the whole must necessarily slip away insensibly, and then you are lost beyond recovery.

2. Let an unaffected gravity, freedom, justice, and sincerity shine through all your actions, and let no

fancies and chimeras give the least check to those excellent qualities. This is an easy task, if you will but suppose everything you do to be your last, and if you can keep your passions and appetites from crossing your reason. Stand clear of rashness, and have nothing of insincerity or self-love to infect you.

3. Manage all your thoughts and actions with such prudence and circumspection as if you were sensible you were just going to step into the grave. A little thinking will show a man the vanity and uncertainty of all sublunary things, and enable him to examine maturely the manner of dying; which, if duly abstracted from the terror of the idea, will appear nothing more than an unavoidable appendix of life itself, and a pure natural action.

4. Consider that ill-usage from some sort of people is in a manner necessary, and therefore don't be disquieted about it, but rather conclude that you and your enemy are both marching off the stage together, and that in a little time your very memories will be extinguished.

5. Among your principal observations upon human life, let it be always one to take notice what a great deal both of time and ease that man gains who is not troubled with the spirit of curiosity, who lets his neighbour's affairs alone, and confines his inspections to himself, and only takes care of honesty and a good conscience.

6. If you would live at your ease, and as much as possible be free from the encumbrances of life, manage but a few things at once, and let those, too, be such as are absolutely necessary. By this rule you will

draw the bulk of your business into a narrow compass, and have the double pleasure of making your actions good, and few into the bargain.

7. He that torments himself because things do not happen just as he would have them, is but a sort of ulcer in the world; and he that is selfish, narrow-souled, and sets up for a separate interest, is a kind of voluntary outlaw, and disincorporates himself from mankind.

8. Never think anything below you which reason and your own circumstances require, and never suffer yourself to be deterred by the ill-grounded notions of censure and reproach; but when honesty and conscience prompt you to say or do anything, do it boldly; never balk your resolution or start at the consequence.

9. If a man does me an injury, what's that to me? 'T is his own action, and let him account for it. As for me, I am in my proper station, and only doing the business that Providence has allotted; and withal, I ought to consider that the best way to revenge is not to imitate the injury.

10. When you happen to be ruffled and put out of humour by any cross accident, retire immediately into your reason, and don't suffer your passion to overrule you a moment; for the sooner you recover yourself now the better you'll be able to guard yourself for the future.

11. Don't be like those ill-natured people that, though they do not love to give a good word to their contemporaries, yet are mighty fond of their own commendations. This argues a perverse and unjust

temper, and often exposes the authors to scorn and contempt.

12. If any one convinces you of an error, change your opinion and thank him for it: truth and information are your business, and can never hurt anybody. On the contrary, he that is proud and stubborn, and wilfully continues in a mistake, 't is he that receives the mischief.

13. Because you see a thing difficult, don't instantly conclude it to be impossible to master it. Diligence and industry are seldom defeated. Look, therefore, narrowly into the thing itself, and what you observe proper and practicable in another, conclude likewise within your own power.

14. The principal business of human life is run through within the short compass of twenty-four hours; and when you have taken a deliberate view of the present age, you have seen as much as if you had begun with the world, the rest being nothing else but an endless round of the same thing over and over again.

15. Bring your will to your fate, and suit your mind to your circumstances. Love your friends and forgive your enemies, and do justice to all mankind, and you'll be secure to make your passage easy, and enjoy most of the comforts that human life is capable to afford you.

16. When you have a mind to entertain yourself in your retirements, let it be with the good qualifications of your friends and acquaintance. Think with pleasure and satisfaction upon the honour and bravery of one, the modesty of another, the generosity of a third,

and so on; there being nothing more pleasant and diverting than the lively images and the advantages of those we love and converse with.

17. As nothing can deprive you of the privileges of your nature, or compel you to act counter to your reason, so nothing can happen to you but what comes from Providence, and consists with the interest of the universe.

18. Let people's tongues and actions be what they will, your business is to have honour and honesty in your view. Let them rail, revile, censure, and condemn, or make you the subject of their scorn and ridicule, what does it all signify? You have one certain remedy against all their malice and folly, and that is to live so that nobody shall believe them.

19. Alas, poor mortals! did we rightly consider our own state and condition, we should find it would not be long before we have forgot all the world, and, to be even, that all the world will have forgot us likewise.

20. He that would recommend himself to the public, let him do it by the candour and modesty of his behaviour, and by a generous indifference to external advantages. Let him love mankind, and resign to Providence, and then his works will follow him, and his good actions will praise him in the gate.

21. When you hear a discourse, let your understanding, as far as possible, keep pace with it, and lead you forward to those things which fall most within the compass of your own observations.

22. When vice and treachery shall be rewarded, and virtue and ability slighted and discountenanced;

when ministers of state shall rather fear man than God, and to screen themselves run into parties and factions; when noise and clamour and scandalous reports shall carry everything before them, 't is natural to conclude that a nation in such a state of infatuation stands upon the brink of destruction, and, without the intervention of some unforeseen accident, must be inevitably ruined.

23. When a prince is guarded by wise and honest men, and when all public officers are sure to be rewarded if they do well, and punished if they do evil, the consequence is plain: justice and honesty will flourish, and men will be always contriving, not for themselves, but for the honour and interest of their king and country.

24. Wicked men may sometimes go unpunished in this world, but wicked nations never do; because this world is the only place of punishment for wicked nations, though not for private and particular persons.

25. An administration that is merely founded upon human policy must be always subject to human chance; but that which is founded on the Divine wisdom can no more miscarry than the government of Heaven. To govern by parties and factions is the advice of an atheist, and sets up a government by the spirit of Satan. In such a government the prince can never be secure under the greatest promises, since, as men's interest changes, so will their duty and affections likewise.

26. It is a very ancient observation, and a very true one, that people generally despise where they flatter, and cringe to those they design to betray; so

that truth and ceremony are, and always will be, two distinct things.

27. When you find your friend in an error, undeceive him with secrecy and civility, and let him see his oversight first by hints and glances; and if you cannot convince him, leave him with respect, and lay the fault upon your own management.

28. When you are under the greatest vexations, then consider that human life lasts but for a moment; and do not forget but that you are like the rest of the world, and faulty yourself in many instances; and withal, remember that anger and impatience often prove more mischievous than the provocation.

29. Gentleness and good-humour are invincible, provided they are without hypocrisy and design; they disarm the most barbarous and savage tempers, and make even malice ashamed of itself.

30. In all the actions of life let it be your first and principal care to guard against anger on the one hand and flattery on the other, for they are both unserviceable qualities, and do a great deal of mischief in the government of human life.

31. When a man turns knave or libertine, and gives way to fear, jealousy, and fits of the spleen; when his mind complains of his fortune, and he quits the station in which Providence has placed him, he acts perfectly counter to humanity, deserts his own nature, and, as it were, runs away from himself.

32. Be not heavy in business, disturbed in conversation, nor impertinent in your thoughts. Let your judgment be right, your actions friendly, and your mind contented; let them curse you, threaten you,

or despise you; let them go on: they can never injure your reason or your virtue, and then all the rest that they can do to you signifies nothing.

33. The only pleasure of human life is doing the business of the creation; and which way is that to be compassed very easily? Most certainly by the practice of general kindness, by rejecting the importunity of our senses, by distinguishing truth from falsehood, and by contemplating the works of the Almighty.

34. Be sure to mind that which lies before you, whether it be thought, word, or action; and never postpone an opportunity, or make virtue wait for you till to-morrow.

35. Whatever tends neither to the improvement of your reason nor the benefit of society, think it below you; and when you have done any considerable service to mankind, don't lessen it by your folly in gaping after reputation and requital.

36. When you find yourself sleepy in a morning, rouse yourself, and consider that you are born to business, and that in doing good in your generation you answer your character and act like a man; whereas sleep and idleness do but degrade you, and sink you down to a brute.

37. A mind that has nothing of hope, or fear, or aversion, or desire, to weaken and disturb it, is the most impregnable security. Hither we may with safety retire and defy our enemies; and he that sees not this advantage must be extremely ignorant, and he that forgets it unhappy.

38. Don't disturb yourself about the faults of

other people, but let everybody's crimes be at their own door. Have always this great maxim in your remembrance, that to play the knave is to rebel against religion; all sorts of injustice being no less than high treason against Heaven itself.

39. Don't contemn death, but meet it with a decent and religious fortitude, and look upon it as one of those things which Providence has ordered. If you want a cordial to make the apprehensions of dying go down a little the more easily, consider what sort of world and what sort of company you'll part with. To conclude, do but look seriously into the world, and there you'll see multitudes of people preparing for funerals, and mourning for their friends and acquaintances; and look out again a little afterwards, and you'll see others doing the very same thing for them.

40. In short, men are but poor transitory things. To-day they are busy and harassed with the affairs of human life, and to-morrow life itself is taken from them, and they are returned to their original dust and ashes.

PART III

Containing prophetic observations relating to the affairs of Europe and of Great Britain, more particularly from 1720 to 1729.

1. In the latter end of 1720, an eminent old lady shall bring forth five sons at a birth; the youngest shall live and grow up to maturity, but the four

eldest shall either die in the nursery or be all carried off by one sudden and unexpected accident.

2. About this time a man with a double head shall arrive in Britain from the south. One of these heads shall deliver messages of great importance to the governing party, and the other to the party that's opposite to them. The first shall believe the monster, but the last shall discover the impostor, and so happily disengage themselves from a snare that was laid to destroy them and their posterity. After this the two heads shall unite, and the monster shall appear in his proper shape.

3. In the year 1721, a philosopher from Lower Germany shall come, first to Amsterdam in Holland, and afterwards to London. He will bring with him a world of curiosities, and among them a pretended secret for the transmutation of metals. Under the umbrage of this mighty secret he shall pass upon the world for some time; but at length he shall be detected, and proved to be nothing but an empiric and a cheat, and so forced to sneak off, and leave the people he has deluded, either to bemoan their loss or laugh at their own folly. *N.B.*—This will be the last of his sect that will ever venture in this part of the world upon the same errand.

4. In this year great endeavours will be used for procuring a general peace, which shall be so near a conclusion that public rejoicings shall be made at the courts of several great potentates upon that account; but just in the critical juncture a certain neighbouring prince shall come to a violent death, which shall occasion new war and commotion all over Europe;

but these shall continue but for a short time, and at last terminate in the utter destruction of the first aggressors.

5. Towards the close of this year of mysteries, a person that was born blind shall have his sight restored, and shall see ravens perch upon the heads of traitors, among which the head of a notorious prelate shall stand upon the highest pole.

6. In the year 1722, there shall be a grand congress, and new overtures of peace offered by most of the principal parties concerned in the war, which shall have so good effect that a cessation of arms shall be agreed upon for six months, which shall be kept inviolable till a certain general, either through treachery or inadvertency, shall begin hostilities before the expiration of the term; upon which the injured prince shall draw his sword, and throw the scabbard into the sea, vowing never to return it till he shall obtain satisfaction for himself, and done justice to all that were oppressed.

7. At the close of this year, a famous bridge shall be broken down, and the water that runs under it shall be tinctured with the blood of two notorious malefactors, whose unexpected death shall make mighty alterations in the present state of affairs, and put a stop to the ruin of a nation, which must otherwise have been unavoidable.

8. 1723 begins with plots, conspiracies, and intestine commotions in several countries; nor shall Great Britain itself be free from the calamity. These shall continue till a certain young prince shall take the reins of government into his own hands; and after

that, a marriage shall be proposed, and an alliance concluded between two great potentates, who shall join their forces, and endeavour, in good earnest, to set all matters upon a right foundation.

9. This year several cardinals and prelates shall be publicly censured for heretical principles, and shall narrowly escape from being torn to pieces by the common people, who still look upon them as the grand disturbers of the public tranquillity, perfect incendiaries, and the chief promoters of their former, present, and future calamities.

10. In 1724-5 there will be many treaties and negotiations, and Great Britain, particularly, will be crowded with foreign ministers and ambassadors from remote princes and states. Trade and commerce will begin to flourish and revive, and everything will have a comfortable prospect, until some desperadoes, assisted by a monster with many heads, shall start new difficulties, and put the world again into a flame; but these shall be but of short duration.

11. Before the expiration of 1725, an eagle from the north shall fly directly to the south, and perch upon the palace of a prince, and first unravel the bloody projects and designs of a wicked set of people, and then publicly discover the murder of a great king, and the intended assassination of another greater than he.

12. In 1726, three princes will be born that will grow up to be men, and inherit the crowns of three of the greatest monarchies in Europe.

13. About this time the Pope will die, and after a great many intrigues and struggles a Spanish car-

dinal shall be elected, who shall decline the dignity, and declare his marriage with a great lady, heiress of one of the chief principalities in Italy, which may occasion new troubles in Europe, if not timely prevented.

14. In 1727, new troubles shall break out in the north, occasioned by the sudden death of a certain prince, and the avarice and ambition of another. Poor Poland seems to be pointed at; but the princes of the south shall enter into a confederacy to preserve her, and shall at length restore her peace, and prevent the perpetual ruin of her constitution.

15. Great endeavours will be used about this time for a comprehension in religion supported by crafty and designing men, and a party of mistaken zealots, which they shall artfully draw in to join with them; but as the project is ill-concerted and will be worse managed, it will come to nothing; and soon afterwards an effectual mode will be taken to prevent the like attempt for the future.

16. 1728 will be a year of inquiry and retrospection. Many exorbitant grants will be reassumed, and several persons who thought themselves secure will be called before the senate, and compelled to disgorge what they have unjustly pillaged either from the crown or the public.

17. About this time a new scaffold will be erected upon the confines of a certain great city, where an old count of a new extraction, that has been of all parties and true to none, will be doomed by his peers to make his first appearance. After this an old lady,

who has often been exposed to danger and disgrace, and sometimes brought to the very brink of destruction, will be brought to bed of three daughters at once, which they shall call Plenty, Peace, and Union; and these three shall live and grow up together, be the glory of their mother, and the comfort of posterity for many generations.

This is the substance of what he either writ or extracted from his papers in the interval between the loss of his speech and the return of his fit, which happened exactly at the time he had computed.

Upon the approach of his fit he made signs to be put to bed, which was no sooner done but he was seized with extreme agonies, which he bore up under with the greatest steadfastness, and after a severe conflict that lasted near eight hours, he expired.

Thus lived and thus died this extraordinary person; a person, though of mean extraction and obscure life, yet when his character comes to be fully and truly known, it will be read with pleasure, profit, and admiration.

His perfections at large would be the work of a volume, and inconsistent with the intention of these papers. I will therefore only add, for a conclusion, that he was a man of uncommon thought and judgment, and always kept his appetites and inclinations within their just limits.

His reason was strong and manly, his understanding sound and active, and his temper so easy, equal, and complaisant, that he never fell out either with men or accidents. He bore all things with the highest affability, and computed justly upon their value and consequence, and then applied them to their proper uses.

A LETTER FROM OXFORD

Sir, — Being informed that you speedily intend to publish some memoirs relating to our dumb countryman, Dickory Cronke, I send you. herewith a few lines, in the nature of an elegy, which I leave you to dispose of as you think fit. I knew and admired the man, and if I were capable, his character should be the first thing I would attempt. — Yours, &c.

AN ELEGY

IN MEMORY OF DICKORY CRONKE, THE DUMB PHILOSOPHER

> Vitiis nemo sine nascitur; optimus ille
> Qui minimis urgetur. — Horace.

If virtuous actions emulation raise,
Then this good man deserves immortal praise.
When Nature such extensive wisdom lent,
She sure designed him for our precedent.
Such great endowments in a man unknown,
Declare the blessings were not all his own,
But rather granted for a time to show
What the wise hand of Providence can do.
In him we may a bright example see
Of nature, justice, and morality;
A mind not subject to the frowns of fate,
But calm and easy in a servile state.
He always kept a guard upon his will,
And feared no harm, because he knew no ill.

THE DUMB PHILOSOPHER;

A decent posture, and an humble mien,
In every action of his life were seen.
Through all the different stages that he went,
He still appeared both wise and diligent:
Firm to his word, and punctual to his trust,
Sagacious, frugal, affable, and just.
No gainful views his bounded hopes could sway,
No wanton thought lead his chaste soul astray.
In short, his thoughts and actions both declare,
Nature designed him her philosopher;
That all mankind, by his example taught,
Might learn to live, and manage every thought.
Oh! could my muse the wondrous subject grace,
And, from his youth, his virtuous actions trace,
Could I in just and equal numbers tell,
How well he lived, and how devoutly fell,
I boldly might your strict attention claim,
And bid you learn, and copy out the man.

J. P.

EXETER COLLEGE, 25th *August* 1719.

EPITAPH

The occasion of this epitaph was briefly thus:— A gentleman, who had heard much in commendation of this dumb man, going accidentally to the churchyard where he was buried, and finding his grave without a tombstone, or any manner of memorandum of his death, he pulled out his pencil, and writ as follows:—

Pauper ubique jacet.

Near to this lonely unfrequented place,
  Mixed with the common dust, neglected lies,
The man that every muse should strive to grace,
  And all the world should for his virtue prize.
  Stop, gentle passenger, and drop a tear,
  Truth, justice, wisdom, all lie buried here.

OR, GREAT BRITAIN'S WONDER

What though he wants a monumental stone,
　　The common pomp of every fool or knave,
Those virtues which through all his actions shone
　　Proclaim his worth, and praise him in the grave.
　　　　His merits will a bright example give,
　　　　Which shall both time and envy, too, outlive.

Oh, had I power but equal to my mind,
　　A decent tomb should soon this place adorn,
With this inscription: Lo, here lies confined
　　A wondrous man, although obscurely born;
　　　　A man, though dumb, yet he was Nature's care,
　　　　Who marked him out her own philosopher.

A TRUE RELATION

OF THE

APPARITION OF ONE MRS. VEAL

THE NEXT DAY AFTER HER DEATH

TO ONE

MRS. BARGRAVE

AT

CANTERBURY, THE 8TH OF SEPTEMBER 1705

THE PREFACE

THIS relation is matter of fact, and attended with such circumstances as may induce any reasonable man to believe it. It was sent by a gentleman, a justice of peace at Maidstone, in Kent, and a very intelligent person, to his friend in London, as it is here worded; which discourse is attested by a very sober and understanding gentlewoman and kinswoman of the said gentleman's, who lives in Canterbury, within a few doors of the house in which the within-named Mrs. Bargrave lives; who believes his kinswoman to be of so discerning a spirit as not to be put upon by any fallacy, and who positively assured him that the whole matter as it is here related and laid down is what is really true, and what she herself had in the same words, as near as may be, from Mrs. Bargrave's own mouth, who, she knows, had no reason to invent and publish such a story, nor any design to forge and tell a lie, being a woman of much honesty and virtue, and her whole life a course, as it were, of piety. The use which we ought to make of it is to consider that there is a life to come after this, and a just God who will retribute to every one according to the deeds done in the body, and therefore to reflect upon our past course of life we have led in the world;

THE PREFACE

that our time is short and uncertain; and that if we would escape the punishment of the ungodly and receive the reward of the righteous, which is the laying hold of eternal life, we ought, for the time to come, to return to God by a speedy repentance, ceasing to do evil and learning to do well, to seek after God early, if haply He may be found of us, and lead such lives for the future as may be well pleasing in His sight.

A RELATION OF THE APPARITION *of* MRS. VEAL

THIS thing is so rare in all its circumstances, and on so good authority, that my reading and conversation has not given me anything like it. It is fit to gratify the most ingenious and serious inquirer. Mrs. Bargrave is the person to whom Mrs. Veal appeared after her death; she is my intimate friend, and I can avouch for her reputation for these last fifteen or sixteen years, on my own knowledge; and I can confirm the good character she had from her youth to the time of my acquaintance; though since this relation she is calumniated by some people that are friends to the brother of Mrs. Veal who appeared, who think the relation of this appearance to be a reflection, and endeavour what they can to blast Mrs. Bargrave's reputation, and to laugh the story out of countenance. But by the circumstances thereof, and the cheerful disposition of Mrs. Bargrave, notwithstanding the unheard-of ill-usage of a very wicked husband, there is not the least sign of dejection in her face; nor did I ever hear her let fall a desponding or murmuring expression; nay, not when actually under her husband's barbarity, which I have been witness to, and several other persons of undoubted reputation.

THE APPARITION OF MRS. VEAL

Now you must know Mrs. Veal was a maiden gentlewoman of about thirty years of age, and for some years last past had been troubled with fits, which were perceived coming on her by her going off from her discourse very abruptly to some impertinence. She was maintained by an only brother, and kept his house in Dover. She was a very pious woman, and her brother a very sober man, to all appearance; but now he does all he can to mull or quash the story. Mrs. Veal was intimately acquainted with Mrs. Bargrave from her childhood. Mrs. Veal's circumstances were then mean; her father did not take care of his children as he ought, so that they were exposed to hardships; and Mrs. Bargrave in those days had as unkind a father, though she wanted neither for food nor clothing, whilst Mrs. Veal wanted for both; so that it was in the power of Mrs. Bargrave to be very much her friend in several instances, which mightily endeared Mrs. Veal; insomuch that she would often say, "Mrs. Bargrave, you are not only the best, but the only friend I have in the world; and no circumstance in life shall ever dissolve my friendship." They would often condole each other's adverse fortune, and read together "Drelincourt upon Death," and other good books; and so, like two Christian friends, they comforted each other under their sorrow.

Some time after, Mr. Veal's friends got him a place in the Custom House at Dover, which occasioned Mrs. Veal, by little and little, to fall off from her intimacy with Mrs. Bargrave, though there was never any such thing as a quarrel; but an indifferency came on by

THE APPARITION OF MRS. VEAL

degrees, till at last Mrs. Bargrave had not seen her in two years and a half; though above a twelve-month of the time Mrs. Bargrave had been absent from Dover, and this last half-year had been in Canterbury about two months of the time, dwelling in a house of her own.

In this house, on the 8th of September last, viz., 1705, she was sitting alone, in the forenoon, thinking over her unfortunate life, and arguing herself into a due resignation to Providence, though her condition seemed hard. "And," said she, "I have been provided for hitherto, and doubt not but I shall be still; and am well satisfied that my afflictions shall end when it is most fit for me;" and then took up her sewing-work, which she had no sooner done but she hears a knocking at the door. She went to see who it was there, and this proved to be Mrs. Veal, her old friend, who was in a riding-habit: at that moment of time the clock struck twelve at noon.

"Madam," says Mrs. Bargrave, "I am surprised to see you, you have been so long a stranger;" but told her she was glad to see her, and offered to salute her, which Mrs. Veal complied with, till their lips almost touched; and then Mrs. Veal drew her hand across her own eyes and said, "I am not very well," and so waived it. She told Mrs. Bargrave she was going a journey, and had a great mind to see her first. "But," says Mrs. Bargrave, "how came you to take a journey alone? I am amazed at it, because I know you have so fond a brother." "Oh," says Mrs. Veal, "I gave my brother the slip, and came

THE APPARITION OF MRS. VEAL

away, because I had so great a desire to see you before I took my journey." So Mrs. Bargrave went in with her into another room within the first, and Mrs. Veal set her down in an elbow-chair, in which Mrs. Bargrave was sitting when she heard Mrs. Veal knock. Then says Mrs. Veal, "My dear friend, I am come to renew our old friendship again, and beg your pardon for my breach of it; and if you can forgive me, you are one of the best of women." "Oh," says Mrs. Bargrave, "don't mention such a thing; I have not had an uneasy thought about it; I can easily forgive it." "What did you think of me?" said Mrs. Veal. Says Mrs. Bargrave, "I thought you were like the rest of the world, and that prosperity had made you forget yourself and me." Then Mrs. Veal reminded Mrs. Bargrave of the many friendly offices she did in her former days, and much of the conversation they had with each other in the time of their adversity; what books they read, and what comfort in particular they received from Drelincourt's "Book of Death," which was the best, she said, on that subject ever wrote. She also mentioned Dr. Sherlock, and two Dutch books which were translated, wrote upon death, and several others; but Drelincourt, she said, had the clearest notions of death and of the future state of any who had handled that subject. Then she asked Mrs. Bargrave whether she had Drelincourt. She said "Yes." Says Mrs. Veal, "Fetch it." And so Mrs. Bargrave goes upstairs and brings it down. Says Mrs. Veal, "Dear Mrs. Bargrave, if the eyes of our faith were as open as the eyes of our body, we should see numbers of angels about us for our guard. The notions we have of heaven now are nothing like what it is, as Drelincourt says. Therefore be comforted under your afflictions, and believe that the Almighty has a particular regard to you, and that your afflictions are marks of God's favour; and when they have done the business they are sent for, they shall be removed from you. And believe me, my dear friend, believe what I say to you, one minute of future happiness will infinitely reward you for all your sufferings; for I can never believe" (and claps her hand upon her knee with great earnestness, which indeed ran through most of her discourse) " that ever God will suffer you to spend all your days in this afflicted state; but be assured that your afflictions shall leave you, or you them, in a short time." She spake in that pathetical and heavenly manner, that Mrs. Bargrave wept several times, she was so deeply affected with it.

Then Mrs. Veal mentioned Dr. Horneck's "Ascetick," at the end of which he gives an account of the lives of the primitive Christians. Their pattern she recommended to our imitation, and said their conversation was not like this of our age; "for now," says she, "there is nothing but frothy, vain discourse, which is far different from theirs. Theirs was to edification, and to build one another up in faith; so that they were not as we are, nor are we as they were; but," said she, "we might do as they did. There was a hearty friendship among them; but where is it now to be found?" Says Mrs. Bargrave, "'T is hard indeed to find a true friend in these days."

THE APPARITION OF MRS. VEAL

Says Mrs. Veal, "Mr. Norris has a fine copy of verses, called 'Friendship in Perfection,' which I wonderfully admire. Have you seen the book?" says Mrs. Veal. "No," says Mrs. Bargrave, "but I have the verses of my own writing out." "Have you?" says Mrs. Veal; "then fetch them." Which she did from above-stairs, and offered them to Mrs. Veal to read, who refused, and waived the thing, saying, holding down her head would make it ache; and then desired Mrs. Bargrave to read them to her, which she did. As they were admiring "Friendship" Mrs. Veal said, "Dear Mrs. Bargrave, I shall love you for ever." In the verses there is twice used the word Elysian. "Ah!" says Mrs. Veal, "these poets have such names for heaven!" She would often draw her hand across her own eyes and say, "Mrs. Bargrave, don't you think I am mightily impaired by my fits?" "No," says Mrs. Bargrave, "I think you look as well as ever I knew you."

After all this discourse, which the apparition put in words much finer than Mrs. Bargrave said she could pretend to, and was much more than she can remember (for it cannot be thought that an hour and three-quarter's conversation could all be retained, though the main of it she thinks she does), she said to Mrs. Bargrave she would have her write a letter to her brother, and tell him she would have him give rings to such and such, and that there was a purse of gold in her cabinet, and that she would have two broad pieces given to her cousin Watson.

Talking at this rate, Mrs. Bargrave thought that a fit was coming upon her, and so placed herself in a chair just before her knees, to keep her from falling to the ground, if her fits should occasion it (for the elbow-chair, she thought, would keep her from falling on either side); and to divert Mrs. Veal, as she thought, she took hold of her gown-sleeve several times and commended it. Mrs. Veal told her it was a scoured silk, and newly made up. But for all this, Mrs. Veal persisted in her request, and told Mrs. Bargrave she must not deny her; and she would have her tell her brother all their conversation when she had an opportunity. "Dear Mrs. Veal," said Mrs. Bargrave, "this seems so impertinent that I cannot tell how to comply with it; and what a mortifying story will our conversation be to a young gentleman!" "Well," says Mrs. Veal, "I must not be denied." "Why," says Mrs. Bargrave, "'t is much better, methinks, to do it yourself." "No," says Mrs. Veal, "though it seems impertinent to you now, you will see more reason for it hereafter." Mrs. Bargrave then, to satisfy her importunity, was going to fetch a pen and ink; but Mrs. Veal said, "Let it alone now, and do it when I am gone; but you must be sure to do it;" which was one of the last things she enjoined her at parting; and so she promised her.

Then Mrs. Veal asked for Mrs. Bargrave's daughter. She said she was not at home, "but if you have a mind to see her," says Mrs. Bargrave, "I'll send for her." "Do," says Mrs. Veal. On which she left her, and went to a neighbour's to send for her; and by the time Mrs. Bargrave was returning, Mrs. Veal was got without the door in the street, in the face of

THE APPARITION OF MRS. VEAL

the beast-market, on a Saturday (which is market-day), and stood ready to part as soon as Mrs. Bargrave came to her. She asked her why she was in such haste. She said she must be going, though perhaps she might not go her journey until Monday; and told Mrs. Bargrave she hoped she should see her again at her cousin Watson's before she went whither she was a-going. Then she said she would take her leave of her, and walked from Mrs. Bargrave in her view, till a turning interrupted the sight of her, which was three-quarters after one in the afternoon.

Mrs. Veal died the 7th of September, at twelve o'clock at noon, of her fits, and had not above four hours' senses before death, in which time she received the sacrament. The next day after Mrs. Veal's appearing, being Sunday, Mrs. Bargrave was mightily indisposed with a cold and a sore throat, that she could not go out that day; but on Monday morning she sends a person to Captain Watson's to know if Mrs. Veal were there. They wondered at Mrs. Bargrave's inquiry, and sent her word that she was not there, nor was expected. At this answer, Mrs. Bargrave told the maid she had certainly mistook the name, or made some blunder. And though she was ill, she put on her hood, and went herself to Captain Watson's, though she knew none of the family, to see if Mrs. Veal was there or not. They said they wondered at her asking, for that she had not been in town; they were sure, if she had, she would have been there. Says Mrs. Bargrave, "I am sure she was with me on Saturday almost two hours." They said it was impossible; for they must have seen her, if

THE APPARITION OF MRS. VEAL

she had. In comes Captain Watson while they are in dispute, and said that Mrs. Veal was certainly dead, and her escutcheons were making. This strangely surprised Mrs. Bargrave, who went to the person immediately who had the care of them, and found it true. Then she related the whole story to Captain Watson's family, and what gown she had on, and how striped, and that Mrs. Veal told her it was scoured. Then Mrs. Watson cried out, "You have seen her indeed, for none knew but Mrs. Veal and myself that the gown was scoured." And Mrs. Watson owned that she described the gown exactly; "for," said she, "I helped her to make it up." This Mrs. Watson blazed all about the town, and avouched the demonstration of the truth of Mrs. Bargrave's seeing Mrs. Veal's apparition; and Captain Watson carried two gentlemen immediately to Mrs. Bargrave's house to hear the relation from her own mouth. And then it spread so fast that gentlemen and persons of quality, the judicious and sceptical part of the world, flocked in upon her, which at last became such a task that she was forced to go out of the way; for they were in general extremely satisfied of the truth of the thing, and plainly saw that Mrs. Bargrave was no hypochondriac, for she always appears with such a cheerful air and pleasing mien, that she has gained the favour and esteem of all the gentry, and 'tis thought a great favour if they can but get the relation from her own mouth. I should have told you before that Mrs. Veal told Mrs. Bargrave that her sister and brother-in-law were just come down from London to see her. Says Mrs. Bargrave, "How came you to order matters so strangely?" "It could not be helped," says Mrs. Veal. And her sister and brother did come to see her, and entered the town of Dover just as Mrs. Veal was expiring. Mrs. Bargrave asked her whether she would drink some tea. Says Mrs. Veal, "I do not care if I do; but I'll warrant this mad fellow" (meaning Mrs. Bargrave's husband) "has broke all your trinkets." "But," says Mrs. Bargrave, "I'll get something to drink in for all that." But Mrs. Veal waived it, and said, "It is no matter; let it alone;" and so it passed.

All the time I sat with Mrs. Bargrave, which was some hours, she recollected fresh sayings of Mrs. Veal. And one material thing more she told Mrs. Bargrave — that old Mr. Breton allowed Mrs. Veal ten pounds a year, which was a secret, and unknown to Mrs. Bargrave till Mrs. Veal told it her. Mrs. Bargrave never varies in her story, which puzzles those who doubt of the truth, or are unwilling to believe it. A servant in a neighbour's yard adjoining to Mrs. Bargrave's house heard her talking to somebody an hour of the time Mrs. Veal was with her. Mrs. Bargrave went out to her next neighbour's the very moment she parted with Mrs. Veal, and told what ravishing conversation she had with an old friend, and told the whole of it. Drelincourt's "Book of Death" is, since this happened, bought up strangely. And it is to be observed that, notwithstanding all this trouble and fatigue Mrs. Bargrave has undergone upon this account, she never took the value of a farthing, nor suffered her daughter to take anything of anybody, and therefore can have no interest in telling the story.

THE APPARITION OF MRS. VEAL

But Mr. Veal does what he can to stifle the matter, and said he would see Mrs. Bargrave; but yet it is certain matter of fact that he has been at Captain Watson's since the death of his sister, and yet never went near Mrs. Bargrave; and some of his friends report her to be a great liar, and that she knew of Mr. Breton's ten pounds a year. But the person who pretends to say so has the reputation of a notorious liar among persons whom I know to be of undoubted repute. Now, Mr. Veal is more a gentleman than to say she lies, but says a bad husband has crazed her; but she needs only to present herself, and it will effectually confute that pretence. Mr. Veal says he asked his sister on her death-bed whether she had a mind to dispose of anything, and she said no. Now, the things which Mrs. Veal's apparition would have disposed of were so trifling, and nothing of justice aimed at in their disposal, that the design of it appears to me to be only in order to make Mrs. Bargrave so to demonstrate the truth of her appearance, as to satisfy the world of the reality thereof as to what she had seen and heard, and to secure her reputation among the reasonable and understanding part of mankind. And then again, Mr. Veal owns that there was a purse of gold; but it was not found in her cabinet, but in a combbox. This looks improbable; for that Mrs. Watson owned that Mrs. Veal was so very careful of the key of her cabinet, that she would trust nobody with it; and if so, no doubt she would not trust her gold out of it. And Mrs. Veal's often drawing her hand over her eyes, and asking Mrs. Bargrave whether her fits had not impaired her, looks to me as if she did it on purpose to remind Mrs. Bargrave of her fits, to prepare her not to think it strange that she should put her upon writing to her brother to dispose of rings and gold, which looked so much like a dying person's request; and it took accordingly with Mrs. Bargrave, as the effects of her fits coming upon her; and was one of the many instances of her wonderful love to her, and care of her, that she should not be affrighted; which indeed appears in her whole management, particularly in her coming to her in the daytime, waiving the salutation, and when she was alone; and then the manner of her parting, to prevent a second attempt to salute her.

Now, why Mr. Veal should think this relation a reflection (as 't is plain he does by his endeavouring to stifle it) I can't imagine, because the generality believe her to be a good spirit, her discourse was so heavenly. Her two great errands were to comfort Mrs. Bargrave in her affliction, and to ask her forgiveness for her breach of friendship, and with a pious discourse to encourage her. So that, after all, to suppose that Mrs. Bargrave could hatch such an invention as this from Friday noon till Saturday noon (supposing that she knew of Mrs. Veal's death the very first moment), without jumbling circumstances, and without any interest too, she must be more witty, fortunate, and wicked too, than any indifferent person, I dare say, will allow. I asked Mrs. Bargrave several times if she was sure she felt the gown. She answered modestly, "If my senses be to be relied on, I am sure of it." I asked her if she heard a sound

THE APPARITION OF MRS. VEAL

when she clapped her hand upon her knee. She said she did not remember she did; and she said, "She appeared to be as much a substance as I did, who talked with her; and I may," said she, "be as soon persuaded that your apparition is talking to me now as that I did not really see her; for I was under no manner of fear; I received her as a friend, and parted with her as such. I would not," says she, "give one farthing to make any one believe it; I have no interest in it. Nothing but trouble is entailed upon me for a long time, for aught I know; and had it not come to light by accident, it would never have been made public." But now she says she will make her own private use of it, and keep herself out of the way as much as she can; and so she has done since. She says she had a gentleman who came thirty miles to her to hear the relation, and that she had told it to a room full of people at a time. Several particular gentlemen have had the story from Mrs. Bargrave's own mouth.

This thing has very much affected me, and I am as well satisfied as I am of the best grounded matter of fact. And why we should dispute matter of fact because we cannot solve things of which we have no certain or demonstrative notions, seems strange to me. Mrs. Bargrave's authority and sincerity alone would have been undoubted in any other case.

THE DESTRUCTION OF THE
ISLE OF ST. VINCENT

The DESTRUCTION OF THE ISLE OF ST. VINCENT

(*From "Mist's Journal," July 5, 1718.*)

WE have a piece of public news this time of such consequence, and so necessary for all our readers to be fully acquainted with, that our friends who have written several letters to us, which otherwise deserve publishing, must excuse us for this week.

This relates to the entire desolation of the island of St. Vincent, in the West Indies, by the immediate hand of Nature, directed by Providence, and in a manner astonishing to all the world, the like of which never happened since the Creation, or, at least, since the destruction of the earth by water in the general Deluge.

Our accounts of this come from so many several hands, and several places, that it would be impossible to bring the letters all separately into this journal; and when we had done so, or attempted to do so, would have the story confused, and the world not perfectly informed. We have therefore thought it better to give the substance of this amazing accident in one collection, making together as full and as distinct account of the whole as we believe is possible to come at by any intelligence whatsoever; and at the close of this account we shall give some proba-

DESTRUCTION OF ST. VINCENT

ble guesses at the natural cause of so terrible an operation. The relation is as follows, viz.:—

An account of the island of St. Vincent, in the West Indies, and of its entire destruction on the 26th of March last, with some rational suggestions concerning the causes and manner of it.

The island of St. Vincent is the most populous of any possessed by the Caribbeans; its latitude is sixteen degrees north from the line. Those who have seen the island Ferro or Fietre, one of the Canaries, affirm that this is much of the same figure. It may be about eight leagues in length, and six in breadth. There are in it several high mountains, and very fruitful plains, if they were cultivated. The Caribbeans have many fair villages, where they live pleasantly, and without any disturbance; and though they have a jealousy of strangers, yet do they not deny them the bread of the country, which is cossava, water, fruits, and other provisions growing in their country, if they want them, taking in exchange wedges, hooks, and other implements of iron, which they much esteem.

On the 24th March a French sloop arrived at Martinico that passed by the island of St. Vincent the 22nd, and, as the master reported, he bought some fish of some of the savages who inhabited there, and who came off to him in three canoes. He says that all was safe and in very good condition there, for anything he perceived, only that some of his seamen report, since the disaster, that one of the Indians told

DESTRUCTION OF ST. VINCENT

them they had been terribly frighted with earthquakes for some time, and with flashes of fire like lightning, which did not come out of the clouds as usual, but out of the earth; and that they had felt these earthquakes for a month past, to their very great amazement.

On the 27th, in the morning, the air was darkened in a dreadful manner; which darkness, by all accounts, seems to have extended over all the colonies and islands which were within 100 miles of the place, but was perceived to be more or less dark as those islands were farther or nearer from the place.

But that which is most remarkable of all is, that at some of the islands, and at Martinico in particular, a dreadful flash of lightning, as they called it, was seen on the 26th about eleven o'clock at night. This flash, which they called lightning, we shall account for in the following part of this relation.

It is to be observed, in the next place, that as there were several ships, or other vessels at sea, in several ports among the islands, some of these had a more terrible sight of this thing than others; particularly they write that in one sloop, which is come into Martinico, the men are so terrified still, and were so amazed at what they saw and heard, that they appear perfectly stupefied, and gave little or no account. Others are come into other ports so horribly frighted that they scarce retain their senses; others give confused accounts, and so, more or less distinct, as they were nearer or farther from the place; the sum of what may be gathered from them all is this:—

That they saw in the night that terrible flash of fire, and after that they heard innumerable clashes of thunder — some say it was thunder they heard — others that it was cannon — only that the noise was a thousand times as loud as thunder or cannon, considering that it appeared to be at a great distance from them.

That the next morning, when the day began to break, the air looked dismally, viz., all overhead was a deep, impenetrable darkness; but below, all round the edge of the horizon, it looked as if the heavens were all on fire. As the day came on, still the darkness increased, till it was far darker than it had been in any part of the night before; and, as they thought, the cloud descended upon them. The darkness still increased after this, viz., in the afternoon they were surprised with the falling of something upon them as thick as smoke, but fine as dust, and yet solid as sand; this fell thicker and faster as they were nearer or farther off — some ships had it nine inches, others a foot thick, upon their decks; the island of Martinico is covered with it at about seven to nine inches thick; at Barbadoes it is frightful, even to St. Christopher's it exceeded four inches; it is fallen over the whole extent of the Isle of Hispaniola, and there is no doubt but it has been seen on the continent of New Spain, about the point of Guiana, or the mouth of the Orinoco; all which will perhaps be accounted for in some measure in the following narrative.

This continued falling for two or three days and nights successively; and it was impossible for any man to find out or so much as guess at the meaning of it, or of any natural cause to produce it, till the whole came to discover itself; but all people stood amazed

DESTRUCTION OF ST. VINCENT

at the cause, and several letters were sent to England of it, from Barbadoes in particular; as of a strange miraculous shower of sand, of which we gave an account in our journal of the 20th past. The first news that was given of the whole thing was by some vessels that were under sail, in the night of the 26th, belonging to Martinico, by which we had the following particulars: that on the said 26th, about midnight, the whole island of St. Vincent rose up into the air, with a most dreadful eruption of fire from underneath the earth and an inconceivable noise in the air at its rising up; that it was not only blown up, but blown out of the very sea, with a dreadful force, as it were torn up by the roots, or blown up from the foundations of the earth.

That the terror was inexpressible, and cannot be represented by words; that the noise of the bursting of the earth at first is not possible to be described; that the force of the blow or blast was such, and the whole body of the island was raised so furiously, that the earth was entirely separated into small particles like dust; and as it rose to an immense height, so it spread itself to an incredible distance, and fell light and gradually, like a small but thick mist. This part, we suppose, must be occasioned by the force of the blow effectually separating the parts, otherwise they would have fallen with a violence of motion, proportioned to the weight of the whole, the particles pressing one another; whereas now every grain was loose and independent in the air, and fell no faster than it was pressed by its own weight, as in a shower of snow or rain.

DESTRUCTION OF ST. VINCENT

The more solid parts of this land, which were lifted up by this blast, and supposed to be of stone, slate, or clay, or such solid matter as would not dissipate or separate in the air, like the rest, being lifted to an immense height, and then plunging, by a mighty force, received by their own weight, into the sea, must of necessity make a noise or blow equal to that of the loudest cannon, and perhaps to thunder itself; and these we think to be the several reports or blows which were heard even to St. Christopher's Island (which is a vast distance from that of St. Vincent), and of which the people in these islands, as well as in the ships, heard about a thousand or twelve hundred distinct blows or reports, and supposed it to be the noise of guns.

As soon as it was understood by the inhabitants in other islands what it was, that is to say, that it was an eruption of the earth at the island of St. Vincent or thereabouts, sloops, barks, and other small vessels came from all parts to see how it was, to inquire into the damage suffered, and to get an account of the particulars; but how astonished must these inquirers be when, meeting from all parts upon the same errand, they may be supposed to go cruising about to find the island, some examining their books to cast up the length they had sailed, some blaming their own negligence for not keeping a right reckoning, some their men for mistaking their distance, others taking observations to know the latitude they were in; at last, all concluding, as it really was, to their great confusion, that the said island was *no more*; that there appeared no remains, except

DESTRUCTION OF ST. VINCENT

three little rocks, no, not any tokens that such an island had been there; but that, on the contrary, in the place of it, the sea was excessive deep, and no bottom to be found at two hundred fathom.

As this is an event so wonderful as no history can give us an account of the like, so it cannot be unpleasant to our readers to consider briefly some natural causes which may be assigned for it.

An earthquake it cannot be — though that is the first thing which offers to our view. Had the island sunk into the water, it had been well enough accounted for in that way; nor are we without examples in history, when earthquakes have raised islands where they had not been seen before, as particularly in the Archipelago, and sunk islands which have been, so that they have been seen no more, as is said of the great island Atlantis, from which some fancy the Atlantic Ocean received its name.

But for an island to be blown up into the air as if it were undermined and blown up by gunpowder, like a bastion in a town besieged, and for the force to be such as to blow up the solid earth into the third region, as we may say — to such a stupendous, prodigious height as to have it go up an island, and come down in sand; to go up in bulk, and come down in atoms; to go up perpendicular, and be spread about to a hundred miles' distance — this is unaccountable but by some force superior to that of ten millions of barrels of gunpowder.

Some, we hear, by casting up the dimensions of the island, to reduce it to cubical inches, are pretending to tell us what weight of earth this blast has raised up, and consequently would tell us what force it was that must raise it; but this is a perfectly needless inquiry, and many ways impracticable also.

But it may not be an unfruitful search if we endeavour to inquire, and offer some probable essay at the manner, how such a wonderful thing as this is in Nature has been, or may be, performed. There seems to be only two several ways for us to conceive of the possibility of such a thing — we mean, by the ordinary course of Nature, and concurrence of causes.

What infinite Power, who made the world, may be supposed to do, we have nothing to say to, nor is it to our purpose in this case to inquire into it.

Infinite Power might as easily blow this whole earth up and dissipate every part of it into the first atoms, from which it may be supposed to have been made, as He could, by the power of His word, form this beautiful figure from the unshaped chaos; but this, we say, is out of the present question.

Our inquiry is into natural and probable causes which might produce such a terrible eruption in Nature as this has been, the like whereof was never heard of before.

First, a concurrence or conjunction of sulphureous and nitrous particles in the subterranean caverns of the earth, of which some might happen to be under this island, of a vast extent, according to the quantity of which particles the force would be; and there's no question but that these particles taking air, by some chasm or vent given to them by some accident of an earthquake or otherwise, might be able to perform this terrible operation.

DESTRUCTION OF ST. VINCENT

As to the nature of an earthquake, it is needless to enter into inquiries here of a thing so well known, or to prove that this might open the hollows and vast caverns in the bowels of the earth, at a great depth, perhaps many hundred fathoms under the bottom of the sea; for as an earthquake effects a dislocation of the parts, it is most natural to suppose it might so open those subterranean hollows, so as to bring air to those particles which were before big with that contracted fire, which, when dilated, would blow up all above them.

The second method in Nature by which this may be supposed to be performed, might be subterranean fires, which, having kindled themselves in the body of the earth, do, in several places, extend themselves to a prodigious space, and often discover to us, more or less, as their magnitude or distance from the surface of the earth may be, sometimes by warming the springs of water which flow near them (from whence our hot baths and warm springs of water are produced), other times by volcanoes or burning mountains, as Mount Gibell or Etna, in Sicily; Mount Vesuvius, near Naples; and Strombolo; Mount Hecla, in Iceland, and the like.

Supposing, then, by the shocks of an earthquake near the cavities where these treasures of fire are reserved, the earth may be opened so as that the sea might come pouring into the vast body of fire, which we may imagine to be kindled there, and which may have burned several hundred years — this, having no vent, would not fail to blow up, not such an island as St. Vincent only, but an island forty times as big in proportion to the extent of the fire below, and to the quantity of water which might come in; and this we believe is the only way we can account for the dreadful eruptions which sometimes happen in those burning mountains mentioned above, and of which we have not room to enlarge here.

The experiment of this may be made familiar by the throwing a pail of water hastily into a furnace — suppose such as a brewer's furnace — which will immediately burst out again, with a violence proportioned to the quantity of water; and, if it were possible, at the same time, to shut the door of the furnace, the force of it would blow up all above it. This also may be illustrated, with great exactness to our imagination, by reflecting on a very sad accident which happened not many years ago in London, and which most people have heard of, viz., at the foundry at Windmill Hill, by Moorfields, where the metal for the casting of a great gun, running into a mould ill prepared, and which had received some water, though by the relation of all concerned in it, and that were alive, that water, by the cavity of the mould, could not be equal to a gallon, yet it blew up the whole work, and blew the melted metal up, as light as if it had been the lightest earth, throwing it about the whole place, separated in small parts like drops, so that it overwhelmed, as with a shower of molten brass, those that were near, and almost all who were in the place were either killed or terribly hurt with it.

We have not room to say any more of this affair

DESTRUCTION OF ST. VINCENT

in this paper: we shall only add, that as by either of these two ways this terrible event of blowing up the island of St. Vincent may be supposed possible in Nature, so we do believe that all the philosophers in the world cannot find a third.

THE END.